Xiaowei Wang

Blockchain Chicken Farm

Xiaowei Wang is an artist, a writer, and a coder. They are the creative director at *Logic* magazine, and their work encompasses community-based and public art projects, data visualization, technology, ecology, and education. Their projects have been finalists for the Index Award and featured by *The New York Times*, the BBC, CNN, *VICE*, and other outlets. They are working toward a Ph.D. at UC Berkeley, where they are a part of the National Science Foundation's Research Traineeship program in Environment and Society: Data Science for the 21st Century.

FSG Originals × *Logic*

FARRAR, STRAUS AND GIROUX

New York

Blockchain Chicken Farm

And Other Stories of Tech in China's Countryside

Xiaowei Wang

FSG Originals × *Logic*
Farrar, Straus and Giroux
120 Broadway, New York 10271

Printed in the United States of America
First edition, 2020

Grateful acknowledgment is made for permission to reprint the following material: Poem from the Alibaba office © Alibaba Cloud, written by Alibaba Cloud engineers.

Library of Congress Cataloging-in-Publication Data
Names: Wang, Xiaowei, 1986– author.
Title: Blockchain chicken farm : and other stories of tech in China's countryside / Xiaowei Wang.
Description: First edition. | New York : Farrar, Straus and Giroux, 2020. | Series: FSG Originals × *Logic* | Includes bibliographical references.
Identifiers: LCCN 2020022509 | ISBN 9780374538668 (paperback)
Subjects: LCSH: Technology—Social aspects—China. | Technology and state—China. | China—Rural conditions. | United States—Commerce—China. | Wang, Xiaowei, 1986– —Travel—China.
Classification: LCC T55.77.C6 W36 2020 | DDC 609.51/091734—dc23
LC record available at https://lccn.loc.gov/2020022509

Our books may be purchased in bulk for promotional, educational, or business use. Please contact your local bookseller or the Macmillan Corporate and Premium Sales Department at 1-800-221-7945, extension 5442, or by e-mail at MacmillanSpecialMarkets@macmillan.com.

www.fsgoriginals.com • www.fsgbooks.com • www.logicmag.io
Follow us on Twitter, Facebook, and Instagram at @fsgoriginals and @logic_magazine

10 9 8 7 6 5 4 3 2 1

Contents

■ ■ ■

Author's Note

The pace of writing a book is slower than the pace of world events. This is a book about technology in China, where change happens particularly fast. Unsurprisingly, many tech companies have been complicit in state violence, persecution, and systemic racism, as well as the silencing of dissent in many regions—including Xinjiang, home to the indigenous Uyghur people. The inclusion of such companies in this book is far from an endorsement. I oppose and condemn all forms of state violence, and I encourage readers to critically engage with the work of scholars and journalists in order to understand the role that tech companies play in maintaining racial capitalism worldwide.

Blockchain Chicken Farm

Introduction

This evening, I am brushing my teeth surrounded by dozens of pin-size black worms that roil and roll along white ceramic tile. A child's socks and underwear are hung out to dry on a small rack next to the sink. It's been raining all day. I'm in a small village in southern China, at the border of Jiangxi and Guangdong. I arrived in the village to try to understand how e-commerce has affected life here, with farmers selling goods directly to consumers, using WeChat's robust mobile payment system. After missing the last bus back to the nearest city, I am now on an involuntary meditation retreat.

Since I'm American, my hosts have assumed I need spacious, extraordinarily comfortable conditions, which is why I'm staying at the most modern house in the village, by myself. It's a two-story concrete building with an outhouse that has a ceramic squat toilet, just a few convenient steps away from the front door.

It's so cold here that I can see my breath inside. There are no radiators, just a small plastic space heater that defeatedly wheezes lukewarm air. It's the only sound I hear besides a low, watery gurgle, accompanied by the wind rattling through cracks of the window frame.

Nighttime is dense and dark here, with no streetlights and few houses, eerily emphasized by the silence of the village. My movements feel muffled and dull. I am unused to this kind of solitude, as someone who spends most of my time in cities, and I am scared—stuck in a new place with only the worms to talk to, maybe a ghost or two, replaying supernatural horror movies in my mind. Without the stimulation of light and sound, my mind turns over thoughts and stories on repeat, revisiting inconsequentially boring past moments like a mantra: Did Xinghai think I was a jerk because I didn't say thank you earlier when he dropped me off? Did I end my e-mail to Gu in the wrong tone? What if I get stuck in this village forever? How slow would I be at harvesting rice? I get bored with my own thoughts and download a night-light app on my phone after scrolling through pages of App Store reviews.

"Why are you here?" One of my hosts, an old rice farmer, asked me this earlier. I had been traveling for days, and in my exhaustion, his question took on a more existential note. It took me a minute before I could sputter, "I'm here to see you."

I felt the pull of rural China about three years ago, after visiting villages in Guizhou, seeing a side of China very different from the one portrayed in most forms of media. This pull was amplified by my need to challenge my own *metronormativity*—a portmanteau of "metropolitan" and "normative," coined by the theorist and scholar Jack Halberstam.

Metronormativity is pervasive—it's the normative, standard idea that somehow rural culture and rural people are backward, conservative, and intolerant, and that the only way to live with freedom is to leave the countryside for highly connected urban oases. Metronormativity fuels the notion that the internet, technology, and media literacy will somehow "save" or "educate" rural people, either by allowing them to experience the broader world, offering new livelihoods, or reducing misinformation.

For me, challenging this metronormativity is crucial. So much of the extended crises and the rise of authoritarian populism throughout the world has been a result of globalization. The urban-rural dynamic is central to globalization, with rural areas serving as the engine, the site of extractive industries from industrial agriculture to rare earth mining. I believe our ability to confront metronormativity will determine our shared future. We are intertwined across cities, villages, and national boundaries, bound by material circumstance.

I have traveled to rare earth and copper mines in Inner Mongolia, driven along dusty highways past wind turbines and data centers, visited villages where artificial intelligence training data is made, and seen empty villages where all the young people have left for electronics factory jobs in cities. Rather than seeing the way technology has shifted or produced new livelihoods in rural China, I have been humbled to see the ways rural China fuels the technology we use every day, around the world.

Questioning metronormativity means demanding something outside the strict binaries of rural versus urban, natural versus man-made, digital versus physical, and remote as disengaged versus metropolitan as connected. To question metronormativity demands a vision of living that serves life itself, and not just life in cities. Embarking on this line of questioning demanded a big change in my own core beliefs.

The dynamics of rural China are not isolated to China itself. Yet because of its geographic distance from the United States, it remains a kind of periphery. These rural peripheries, the edges of the world, hidden from view, enable our existence in cities. These areas produce everything from the cotton in the clothes we wear to the minerals that create the computers in data centers. They also produce the food we eat. It is impossible to disentangle the countryside from food—food is at the core of the dynamic between the rural and the global. As humans, we eat to survive, and our appetite for food has carved new geographies and technologies into the world. Urbanite appetites, especially, have shifted rural economies, ecologies, and societies over the past three decades.

I have a difficult time grasping the full dynamics of complex concepts like climate change, which creates economic and ecological relationships at a dizzying array of scales throughout the world. Yet agriculture and what we eat are tangible manifestations of these entangled global issues that affect all of us. According to a recent United Nations report, a third of human greenhouse gas emissions stem from industrial agricultural practices. These same industrial agriculture practices have rearranged the way rural communities live, fomenting political change around the world.

Conducting research in rural China meant that I could, selfishly, return to villages that I love being in. There was an allure to living at a pace and scale that felt comprehensible, to living in a place that felt grounded. It is easy to romanticize rural Chinese villages as idyllic scenes of nature, small and disengaged—yet many of them are sites of economies and agricultural practices that are foundational to our world. And as numerous historians, such as Robert Brenner and Sue Headlee, have shown, shifts in agriculture and rural politics were crucial for the transition into industrialization and capitalism throughout the world. In thinking through agriculture, through a sense of place and belonging, I was influenced by the writings of bell hooks and Wendell Berry, for whom being and belonging acquire a sense of urgency—especially in a political and economic system that dislocates people from place and community. It would have been easy to attribute the loss of belonging, of place, to just technology accelerating us into the singularity of despondency. But challenging my metronormativity meant challenging these ideas of the digital world versus the physical world, and pulling back the idea that becoming a Luddite and disengaging is the only way to reclaim a sense of belonging.

"Why are you here?" I am here because looking at technology in rural China, in places that produce the technology we use, places that show how globally entangled we are with one another, allows me to confront the scarier question that technology poses: What does it mean to live, to be human right now? Looking at tech in rural China forced me to examine the ideologies that drive engineers and companies to build everything from AI farming systems and blockchain food projects to shopping sites and payment platforms. These assumptions about humans and the way the world *should* work are more powerful than sheer technical curiosity in driving the creation of new technologies and platforms. Embedded in these tools are their makers' and builders' assumptions about what humans need, and how humans *should* interact. It is not enough to critique these assumptions, because in simply critiquing, we remain caught in the long list of binaries: Tech is dehumanizing, tech brings liberation. Tech dragged the world into the mess it's in, tech frees it from this mess. Tech creates isolation, tech connects marginalized communities. The difficult work that we face is to live and thrive beyond binaries and assumptions, and to aid and enable others to do so. How do we begin this work?

At the age of ninety-five, five years before her death, the activist Grace Lee Boggs wrote *The Next American Revolution*. Published in 2010, the book sounded an alarm bell for our present condition—a time when politics was no longer politics as usual, where traditional forms of protest were not enough to induce change, and when ecological disaster wrought by unfettered material and technological growth was looming. Despite all this, she pointed to a source of hope: "the great turning." The great turning, a term borrowed from Buddhism, refers to a growing tidal wave of people now taking the first step toward change: addressing spiritual impoverishment. "These are the times to grow our souls," she writes. The way to respond to crisis is to practice compassion and change the cycle of suffering. We can all actively practice compassion in our own way, whether we are doctors, teachers, or businesspeople. Engineers and makers and builders of technology have this opportunity; I hope this book sparks something for you. After all, code is words made executable—we must take care in what we say. And for those of us who see code as an apocryphal text, who see technology as indeed accelerating us toward a despondent, tightly controlled world, I hope this book reaffirms the power that you hold in *being human*, and demonstrates ways certain technologies might actually serve open systems. To spark the great turning, we need to transform our compassion, our imagination, and our society—we cannot focus on reforming our technologies alone. Most of all, I hope that this book brings you to parts of China that you might never visit, takes you beyond a map of abstractions, a flat map made by metronormativity.

At some point on my involuntary meditation retreat, I start to panic. I have my phone, there's 4G service, and, trying to combat the dark, I scroll Twitter, read the news, peruse my WeChat feed. Against the heaviness of the night, the oppressive immediacy of the cold and quiet, and the lurking outhouse worms, the words on the *New York Times* website feel far away, flimsy. My thoughts feel flimsy.

With my phone screen on, set to my new night-light app, I finally begin drifting into sleep.

In the morning, the scarce winter light starts to shine at 7:00 a.m. I wake to a different world, one that is much less scary, much less sinister than my mind had imagined, at night, in silence. I hear the sounds of ducks and chickens, a single car in the distance. After tidying up the house, I walk past rice paddies and a small stream to the main road. I stand, waiting for the bus.

.1.

Ghosts in the Machine

1.

Famine has its own vocabulary, a hungry language that haunts and lingers. My ninety-year-old great-uncle understands famine's words well. When I visit him one winter, he takes me on an indulgent trip to the food court near his house, at Tianjin's Kerry Center. He has a small, tidy pension that he spends sparingly; he never goes out to eat. Yet he says my visit is special, so I know his affection will be communicated through food, from his own memory of hunger—an endless selection of dishes await us at the mall.

We walk from his apartment. His gait is still brisk from more than seventy years of *taiji* practice. Along the way, we pass a skeletal skyscraper under construction, concrete guts spilling out.

"Wasn't that under construction last time I was here, five years ago?" I ask. It's rare for a building to be under construction for so long in contemporary China, especially in a big city like Tianjin that has been absorbed into the greater Beijing metropolis.

My great-uncle's gaze travels up the skyscraper. "That building was put up by a real estate developer, he's the son of a rich guy. After Xi Jinping's anti-corruption campaign, the developer got caught and the building was confiscated. The government wanted to continue the project and finish the building. But when they looked closely at the plans, they found that the size of each apartment was completely uninhabitable. Living rooms that were smaller than four square meters, windows that faced walls . . . the developer never planned on having people live in there at all. So now it just stands here, half constructed."

It's a Tuesday, and the food court in the mall is empty, with a few other elderly people eating by themselves. There's something casually heartbreaking about the whole scene: fluorescent lights and the occasional "Hello, welcome!" disembodied robot voice on repeat, triggered by a faulty motion sensor. A white-haired man sits at one plastic table, a cloth wallet hanging from a string around his neck, eating a bowl of noodles, slouching in a sleepy nearness to death. At another table, a woman is drinking juice, a folded napkin stuck to the plastic cup, the corners of her mouth drooping with age. On weekends, the food court is crowded with young families from nearby residential buildings, but on weekdays this court is the dominion of the old. And in contemporary China, this is a common plague, the plague of being old and lonely. As younger generations leave villages, hometowns, even the country itself to chase after careers and jobs, and the tightening noose of income inequality squeezes leisure time, the elderly are left to their own devices. This is unusual for a culture so focused on family and filial piety.

I do not know the language of famine, but under fluorescent lights at a table of spicy, numbing vegetables, dumplings, and noodles on plastic dishes, it's clear that my great-uncle is well acquainted with it. "Eat." He gestures. And so I eat, even though we both know that what we're eating is essentially junk food, that there's still food waiting for us in the refrigerator at home, that we've ordered too much. But it doesn't matter, because after you have encountered famine, indulgence is being able to throw away any scrap of food.

2.

During my visit to Tianjin, I see how the landscape of urban, contemporary China can be difficult to square with its past. This tension is what so many Western writers and media draw on: the seduction of contradiction. They conjure images of modern, gleaming skyscrapers alongside ramshackle food stalls, the chaos of crowds tracked by surveillance cameras, the steam from a wok reflecting the blue light of an iPhone. While these images are true in one dimension, I dislike them just as much as I dislike certain types of books on China that compress history into simple demographic change, or economic cause and effect. Such images and forms obscure life through a dense veil of figures, playing on the symbols that already exist in your mind. A kind of numerical inhumanity takes over.

The way images of the East shape political policy in the West has persisted throughout history. "When will the West understand, or try to understand, the East? We

Asiatics are often appalled by the curious web of facts and fancies which has been woven concerning us. We are pictured as living on the perfume of the lotus, if not on mice and cockroaches," wrote Kakuzo Okakura in 1906.[1] Surface images and histories are easily transformed into the ever-present anxieties about "yellow peril" that I see in the United States, and which infiltrates government policy and everyday life.

As my great-uncle stares out the window of his apartment, he unravels a different kind of history, meandering through his memories. He now lives a quiet life of routine, between morning *taiji* practice and occasional phone calls with an old friend. He recalls falling in love with his wife when he was a tuberculosis patient at a hospital in Beijing—she was a doctor there. He recounts his wife's turbulent life; deemed a class enemy by the Communists, her father fled to Taiwan, and her two siblings committed suicide after becoming targets of anti-Rightist campaigns. He turns to me, profile outlined by the low winter sun, and says, "I know you're here writing a book about Chinese technology, but the only way to understand China's future is through its past." What I think he means to say is that the weight of lived history is unshakable, and it will haunt you, whether you are an ordinary citizen or in the upper echelons of power. At his age, he will be talking to you in the present moment when stories from the past suddenly swell up without warning. Sometimes they are stories of *jiushehui*, or the old society, a common term used by the Chinese Communist Party for pre-1949 China, a weak China unable to define a future for itself.

My grandmother had her own stories of *jiushehui*. She

described living in a village outside Tianjin as a child and the hard labor of picking river rushes to braid baskets that she sold at town markets. She remembered her mother's tiny bound feet, how her father and other men in the village were always absent, conscripted into one war or another. The way hunger made you dizzy, seeing stars in daylight. It was this bare existence that led her family to migrate to the city of Tianjin in search of a stability that did not rely on seasons and harvests. Tianjin was still divided into parcels belonging to Western powers at the time. My great-uncle was the doorboy at a Western restaurant; pale white men and women moved past him, their dress and demeanor exuding power. Unlike so many children of that time, he not only survived famine by eating restaurant leftovers but would eventually be able to attend school, funded by my grandmother's income as a factory girl.

The past confronted my grandmother constantly in the way she was unable to tell her personal stories without talking about political events. These political events physically shaped her—she lived most of her life on crutches, one leg having been amputated during the Cultural Revolution after faulty medical advice from a young student while the country's doctors and intellectuals were being "reeducated" in the countryside. Growing up, I would hear my grandmother sleep-talking in her bedroom next to mine. Some nights, she would reenact the past in her dreams. In the darkness, ghosts would emerge and I'd wake to her wails—"Leave me alone, you foreign devil!" In the morning I would ask her about her dreams, and she would reply, with a blank look, that she could not remember them at all.

3.

The third day of my visit involves watching several hours of TV with my great-uncle. There's a dramatic, true-story special about a young village kid who was raised by his grandmother. After heading to the big city with his older brother, he was kidnapped and doomed to a life of hard labor. Twenty years later, he's on live TV being reunited with his grandmother. I turn my head and see my great-uncle sniffling and crying at the show.

Other programs are aimed at the elderly daytime audience. A talk show on health and medicine features an old man showing off his technique for battling constipation: dressing up in a raincoat and blow-drying his stomach until he sweats. Two doctors, one a Western medicine specialist and the other a Chinese medicine practitioner, sit in front of a painted landscape debating the effectiveness of the tactic. An ad comes on that reminds viewers of our "Core Socialist Values." Hours later, I watch the evening news report, a deflated affair filled with some world events and party propaganda. In one segment, the TV anchor heads to a bus station, interviewing migrant workers about buying bus tickets to go home. One worker is not optimistic about his chances of getting a bus ticket during the upcoming Spring Festival, or Chun Yun (春运), one of the world's busiest travel seasons.

During the Chinese Spring Festival, a multiweek affair, a travel frenzy descends across the country. In 2018, nearly three billion trips were made over the monthlong period, many by people headed to their ancestral homes (*laojai*, 老家) in the countryside, or by rural migrants returning home. Returning to your ancestral home is not just a return to the earth, to soil, but a time to visit elders and extended family. Your ancestral home is often where your *hukou*, or household registration, is, part of a government system that incentivizes people to stay in certain geographical areas.

If you were lucky enough to be born in Beijing, you'd receive a Beijing *hukou* and numerous benefits, including access to almost fully reimbursed health care in Beijing, home to some of the best hospitals in the country. You'd also receive education for your children at top schools, and they'd be given a lower bar for standardized test scores to get into the country's top universities, Tsinghua and Beida (Peking University). On the other hand, if you have a *hukou* in a rural area, you are given a title to a piece of land you can farm, which technically you are stewarding for the government. If you do decide to migrate to the city, your children's access to Beijing's wonderful schools is limited. The amount you get reimbursed for a hospital visit in Beijing is next to nothing, and if you did have dreams of upward mobility by attending Tsinghua or Beida, you'd have to outrank native Beijingers on standardized tests, all the while harboring little hope that you'd be one of the lucky few to bypass the *hukou*-based admissions quotas at these schools. Despite all these disincentives to leave, more than three hundred million people have left their rural homes in search of work in nearby cities, creating China's economic miracle over the past thirty years. Such rural migrants take jobs that urbanites refuse—from making iPhones in a Foxconn factory to building the awe-inspiring Olympic architecture of Beijing. In modern China, the peasant turned migrant worker is always haunting the landscape, in skyscrapers and cell phones, in the welded tracks of bullet trains. Without the rural population, contemporary China would not be what it is today.

The *hukou* system reveals the unabashed directness of socialist central planning. There is no dark magic like the American Dream, a sugarcoating that lets you believe in an imagined freedom, when really, the way we have structured our capitalist economy in the United States also relies on distinct labor and class differences. In central planning, rural laborers and peasants must efficiently produce food to feed the nation, to sustain a knowledge-based workforce in cities.

The rural peasant has always been a foundational, central figure in China's nation building. After World War II, during China's civil war, Mao Zedong's winning strategy against the Kuomintang was to catalyze China's peasantry. Peasants would lead his revolution, "encircling cities from the countryside" (农村包围城市).

During the Great Leap Forward, Mao attempted to collectivize farming, with disastrous results. The country embarked on an attempt at industrialization—through almost laughable means, including village steel furnaces where farmers smelted agricultural tools into useless pig iron. Mao and others in power had an anti-elite, anti-intellectual attitude, insisting that technology was a tool for peasants and the people, unveiling programs with names like Mass Scientific Research in Agricultural Villages. For the early nation, technology was an ideology for achieving an imagined future, a future that already existed in the West.

Mao's economic plans were aimed at matching Western industrial and agricultural production in sheer volume, from steelmaking to grain farming. The early project of building a socialist nation demanded a mass fervor for fighting Western imperialism and, most important, the rewriting of a national story to weave a new consciousness. Yet the West would still haunt China, serving as an image on which to project all the early nation's ambitions and rivalries.

The attempts at catching up were troubled. The famine of the Great Leap Forward was devastating, with millions of deaths in the countryside. After the Great Leap Forward, a food coupon system was used throughout the country, controlling how much food each family could purchase—rice, grains, eggs, and meat. The system was a mechanism by the government to control urban consumption, agricultural prices, and yields. The food coupons would be used all the way into the 1990s.

Beginning in the 1980s, technology shifted from a means of survival to a way of imagining a uniquely Chinese future. The country's policies changed drastically, as Deng Xiaoping presided over the combination of free market strategies and socialism: socialism with Chinese characteristics. China's economy boomed, laying the foundation for companies like Huawei and Alibaba.

The countryside became an economic incubator in this ambitious experiment. Both Jean C. Oi, a Stanford political scientist, and the MIT economist Yasheng Huang emphasize the importance of Town and Village Enterprises (TVEs) in the 1980s. It was these enterprises that marked the "rural roots of Chinese capitalism," writes Huang.[2] According to

Huang, rural residents from some of the poorest provinces were undertaking bold entrepreneurship that was impossible in cities. These entrepreneurial models, TVEs, were radically different from the government-controlled State Owned Enterprises (SOEs). Instead, TVEs were a decisively indigenous innovation, centered around local, village-level decision-making—an *agile* environment of sorts. By 1995, "TVEs accounted for approximately a quarter of China's GDP, two-thirds of the total rural output . . . and more than one-third of China's export earnings."[3] And with this economic boom, free market socialism allowed for another kind of national consciousness to emerge. Rather than being at the whim of other countries' political events, global stirrings, and European treaties, perhaps China might gain the freedom to define a future on its own terms—the kind of power that had long been afforded to Western countries.

The desire for this kind of national autonomy not only fuels Chinese nationalism but also makes it crucial for China to demonstrate technological prowess and economic might. Nationalism has led to a small group of leaders wielding tight control over the country, claiming that strong leadership is necessary to China's freedom on a global stage. Yet the irony is, freedom will always slip away when grasped too firmly.

4.

The People's Republic of China was founded October 1, 1949, and is twenty years younger than my great-uncle. The nation's comparatively young age is a reminder to those in power of the ways upheaval is a constant possibility, and that any perception of fragility must be wiped away.

This same fragility breeds nationalist strategies of technological self-reliance, like the Made in China 2025 strategic plan to cultivate China's knowledge industries, alongside a firm focus on the countryside as a place of technological growth. While the countryside and agriculture may seem antithetical to the project of industrialization and high-tech work, the balancing act that China is currently undertaking emphasizes how intertwined the rural and urban are, with technological change threaded throughout. What China faces now is a potential "agrarian transition," a term used by economists and agricultural policy makers. Agrarian transition is the process in which farmers are pushed out of the countryside and small-scale farming is replaced by industrialized agriculture, which requires less manual labor. As a result, there is a surplus of labor as farmers attempt to re-skill or find new jobs.

The same thing occurred during the Industrial Revolution in the West. As the agronomist Eric Holt-Giménez describes, technologies such as the steam engine, mills, and the telegraph were only partially responsible for industrialization and capitalism. Labor, especially factory labor, played an equally important role, and the Industrial Revolution "could have never happened without the agrarian transition. The Industrial Revolution displaced people from the countryside and created a large reserve army of labor."[4] While the transition might sound easy or logical, the social, environmental, and political ramifications of an agrarian transition are enormous. And after such transitions, when development in urban areas reaches new kinds of peaks, labor finds ways to expand and transform under a free market.

Despite threats of China's economic development overshadowing the economy of the United States, the future of China remains as precarious as ever, balancing rural-urban dynamics and the ever-increasing materialism of urban life. During one conversation I had, a Chinese government policy adviser said to me, "I definitely wouldn't want to be in power right now. There's so many cascading problems, it's not a fun position to be in. And the people in power are very aware of these problems."

There is an urgency to build the new socialist countryside in response to these problems. While the term "the new socialist countryside" has existed since 2006 (coined by President Hu Jintao, Xi Jinping's predecessor), Xi Jinping's recent policies of Rural Revitalization have taken a much bolder stance in addressing hollowed-out villages and rural decline. These policies affect nearly 40 percent of the national population (8 percent of the world's total population), who live in the countryside.

The new socialist countryside will be filled with peasants starting e-commerce businesses, small-scale manufacturing, new data centers, and young entrepreneurial workers returning to their rural homes. Rural Revitalization envisions the use of blockchain and mobile payment to catalyze new businesses, and will leverage big data for poverty relief and distribution of welfare benefits.

Numerous government policies, including poverty alleviation efforts, have laid the groundwork for Rural Revitalization. Rural Revitalization prioritizes China's food security by sustaining at least 124 million hectares of arable land—what the government calls maintaining the "red line." The Made in China 2025 plan comprises industrial policies that include homegrown farm-machinery manufacturing and the stabilization of food production. Closely associated with the goal of poverty alleviation is the desire to create new consumers (and internet users) through a rural "consumption upgrade," where the hope is that rural internet users will become full-fledged online shoppers. China Mobile and China Unicom have rolled out feats of infrastructural magic, including 4G and 5G cell service to remote regions. Small rural entrepreneurs are being cultivated by tech monopolies like the e-commerce platforms Alibaba and JD.com.

As I talked to policy advisers and looked at Rural Revitalization documents, I couldn't help but compare them to American rural policies. Back home, driving down the California I-5, which cuts through the agricultural Central Valley, always reveals San Francisco as being a kind of urban delusion. Along the I-5 is a procession of Amazon fulfillment warehouses, resource extraction sites, industrial agriculture, communities ravaged by the Farm Crisis of the 1980s, and prisons—one of the biggest industries in the rural United States, and growing ever larger. A 2001 article from *The New York Times* about economic revitalization in rural America said that building prisons was more effective than building Walmarts or meatpacking plants in stimulating economic growth. As the abolitionist and scholar Ruth Wilson Gilmore writes in her book *Golden Gulag: Prisons,*

Surplus, Crisis, and Opposition in Globalizing California, prisons were purposefully constructed in rural California throughout the 1990s with an economic agenda. The rural prison industry was fueled by policy makers trying to alleviate the economic crisis, because even as crime rates declined across America, prison populations grew. Building rural prisons would capitalize on the surplus foreclosed land that came from the Farm Crisis, and transfer vulnerable urban communities of color into rural prisons just as the social services of education, health care, and public assistance were being eroded. A 2017 study by the Vera Institute of Justice highlighted how the rural incarceration trend continues to grow. According to the study, financial incentives encourage the building of more rural prisons, and thousands of rural prisons are expanding their capacity—despite drastically declining crime rates and growing evidence that rural prison industries fuel national sociopolitical upheaval.

The sociopolitical upheaval in China after the Great Leap Forward and the wild uncertainty of the current U.S. political climate both stand as lessons to China's current lawmakers: agrarian transition is enormously tricky and the consequences are huge, especially in an era of global agricultural trade. Although China harbors dreams of becoming an AI superpower, the question of the countryside will have to be resolved in order for China to garner enough knowledge workers.

China has one of the largest rates of income inequality in the world, due to the rural-urban income gap. Rural migrants work for little pay in cities but are unable to actually stay in urban areas. Yet *hukou* system reform is beginning, although there are new signs that rural *hukou* holders are less enthusiastic about switching to urban *hukous*.[5] China's land reform has continued by allowing farmers to lease out their land or transfer land rights to another, enabling an extra source of income. And as China is a country built on experiments, Rural Revitalization just might succeed in creating sustainable growth in the countryside. The constitutionally sanctioned Organic Law of Villages allows villagers to democratically elect their governing committees, which in some places has resulted in villagers holding those in power more accountable for social and economic well-being. The agricultural tax on peasants was abolished in 2006, allowing more investment opportunity, and the slow trickle of migrants back to the countryside has brought an influx of knowledge and technology.[6]

The cultural differences between the city and the countryside can still be felt. This might be best encapsulated in the frequent stories of rural citizens stealing from the Chinese state government: bemused journalists describe the theft of state electricity wires, concrete, and other building materials that are then resold on illicit markets. In Shandong Province, I asked one thief why they decided to steal from the government. As if I were missing the obvious, they responded, "Well, clearly I would never steal from other villagers and none of the villagers would steal from me. We all know each other. Once in a while, we'll take vegetables from each other's gardens. But anything of value, I'd steal from someone I don't know!"

5.

One night, I decide to cook a simple shrimp dish for my great-uncle. Fifty years ago, shrimp would have been difficult to come by, but these days it's as easy as going to the supermarket and paying via mobile phone. As we eat, my great-uncle reminisces about the early days of the revolution, how at the time, leaders of the Communist Party dressed and ate the same as regular civilians. About how slow work was, how time moved differently then—a filmy haze seemed to cover every moment, suspending life in the present.

In his 1947 book, *From the Soil*, the sociologist Fei Xiaotong underscores the agricultural roots of Han Chinese culture and shows how distinct values emerged in rural areas. In Fei's eyes, rural culture is marked by a different sense of time, a different cosmology. At the core of rural culture, he says, is a belief that the universe is already perfect as it is, and that our duty as humans is to maintain that harmony. This was a sentiment I heard often from farmers as I traveled throughout the countryside. One farmer told me that the future is a created concept, and that in the fields, in the long dark of winters, there is no future, because every day depends on tending to the present moment. An act of care. In contrast, urban culture is centered on the belief that the universe must be constantly corrected on its course, and that life is defined by the pleasure of overcoming future challenges.

On this winter night, as I sit across from my great-uncle, he's tapping away on his WeChat—the Chinese messaging app made by Tencent that has ballooned to include a plethora of other functions, including mobile payment and numerous internal apps, a secondary set of platforms embedded inside WeChat called "mini programs." The last time I had visited both him and my great-aunt, who was still in good health, was 2009. I was living in Beijing at the time. The high-speed train between Beijing and Tianjin had just been completed a year prior, shortening an hour-and-a-half journey to thirty minutes. None of us had smartphones then. Without the watchful weight of a screen in my pocket, a device anchoring and tracking my movements, I floated, as *beipiao*—a drifter like millions of other migrants who moved to Beijing seeking a future. Fewer screens and fewer surveillance cameras meant I was free to spend late nights wandering along Chang'an Avenue, past Mao's mausoleum, through the *hutong* alley bars that had not yet been dismantled, past the vegetable sellers who still lined Beijing's narrow streets and the windows of migrant workers' homes that were still intact, unbroken by police.

The easy argument is that the world is moving faster, becoming more controlled because of the internet and mobile devices. But the gravity of acceleration is not inevitable. The way we experience time has changed; the kind of critical wonder we hold toward objects has collapsed. My great-uncle once sat in amazement looking at the new Japanese-made TV we bought him, at how crisp the image was, and how remarkable it was that so much complex circuitry could fit inside a thin screen. He now looks up from his smartphone occasionally, complaining how slow his phone is at opening apps.

While he's busy sending Toutiao news articles to his friends, I look at my own device. The darkened screen beckons to me, reflecting back like an ancient scrying mirror, a device used for divination, a mirror on which to project all our desires. The future, in perpetuity. One of the gifts of the free market has been precisely that: the delusion that we are free of the past, expanding ever outward into a startling, wild future abetted by the free market, liberalism, and technology. The end of history, as Francis Fukuyama would call it. I have traded a family story, subject to the forces of political will, for a life that changes and moves under economic forces, through the will of financial capital, of Alibaba and Amazon. And it remains to be seen just how the inhabitants of the new socialist countryside will embrace this same free market futurity.

As I stare harder into my blank screen, I realize I don't see the future of the internet, of technology, the future of China's place in the world, but simply the place where I am now: Tianjin, a city that was always subject to global forces, simple geographies, degrees separated from its past. I see Tianjin's port, the Haihe River winding through the city to the ocean, and how the skyscrapers gleam against the glassy waves of the Bohai Sea. Tianjin, as it is, a place that does not have to be read in relation to someone else's history. No single vision of an imagined nation, no single person staking a claim to dictate everyone's future, either on this side of the Pacific or the other. I see so clearly the constant mental images nations have or make of each other. A world politics based on mirrors. What is China but a projection of American fears and desires? And for China, what is the United States but a projection of desires and fears? Nationalist dreams stand, dull and mute, nothing more than a point between dream and illusion. There is nothing to be gained by dreaming, and everything to be gained by seeing.

How to Feed an AI

How would moving beyond machine-human boundaries and Western models of mind-body dualism bring new life to AI research? This recipe speculates on just that—when a group of AI researchers use traditional Chinese medicine, a five-thousand-year-old system of medical practices and philosophy, to advance technology. It is not new for proposals for eating and nutrition to be foundational to philosophy, from the core tenets of Taoism and Buddhism to works on macrobiotic diets by George Ohsawa and Aveline Kushi. Seeing the body as a holistic system, non-Western theories of the body allow for new ways of thinking through substance, matter, and being, which are core to the project of building sentient artificial intelligence. These non-Western theories have been marginalized throughout time by the forces of imperialism and colonialism.

Ingredients

dong quai (*Angelica sinensis*) | 9 g

goji berries | 9 g

ginger, cut into coarse slices | 16 g

whole red dates, chopped | 12

soy milk | 2,000 ml

uncooked white rice | 200 g
dried apricots, diced | 100 g

While companies in the West promised self-driving cars and fully sentient machines by 2020, neural networks used in AI are still constrained by a number of factors, including the specificity of training data for AI models, which is said to create a "generalization problem": an inability to adapt to unseen new data. For example, AI models trained to perform facial recognition can classify well-lit images with great accuracy, but have a difficult time classifying faces if the photos are obscured, occluded, or shown in different lighting conditions than the images on which the AI model was trained. This barrier, along with increasing techno-pessimism, led to a decreased public interest in AI.

In the midst of winter 2022, when venture capital funding and public enthusiasm for AI dried up, a group of Chinese scientists and researchers at the Alibaba AI lab took up the task of generalizing AI models. Instead of Western philosophies of mind, they started from Chinese theories of the body, Chinese medicine, and Buddhist thought. In Western medicine, models of the body center around the brain, which controls other organs, the processes that regulate our body, consciousness, and emotion. In Chinese medicine, there are eleven vital organs that work holistically to sustain life, and this list does not include the brain. Brain functions are scattered throughout the body.

Researchers managed to create a pretrained neural network with electrical inputs and outputs from a combination of artificial and human organs. This hybrid machine was able to perform broader tasks without further training data; however, it was still not fully sentient. Scientists believe further development is needed to better understand what other parts of the body creative and language functions reside in. Yet the ability of the machine to extend its thinking was the first breakthrough in a long, icy AI winter.

The system did not have access to typical conduits for qi (the defining force in Chinese medicine), such as hair, skin, or muscle, to send to the machine-meat hybrid. In order to nourish this system of organs and neural networks, it had to be constantly fed tonifying food: foods to nourish the vital organs in the system.

This porridge was developed by researchers to nourish and tonify the system. It's quick and easy to make. You can use a pressure cooker, an Instant Pot, or a rice cooker with a porridge setting. Make sure the rice-to-soy-milk ratio is 1:10. After that, put in the other ingredients (dong quai, goji berries, ginger, red dates, dried apricots). Bring the mixture to a boil and then simmer for 1 hour, or run the porridge setting on your Instant Pot.

.2.

On a Blockchain Chicken Farm in the Middle of Nowhere

1.

There is a cell phone service blackout in the city of Zhenjiang on the day I visit the Vinegar Culture Museum. As I leave the bullet train station, I frantically tap my ride-hailing app, DiDi, in hopes that some car will show up on the screen. My phone doesn't have 4G or even 3G, just a puny little one-bar signal, for emergency calls.

It's a balmy day in Zhenjiang, a small city outside Nanjing, the old imperial capital for the Ming dynasty, before Beijing was even on a map. During childhood trips to China, my mental categorization of places was based on whether or not a city had a McDonald's, an approximation of the "tiered city" system. Throughout China, the tiered city system is like an economic badge, calculated by a mystical formula that takes in the city's contribution to GDP, average monthly incomes, and housing prices. First-tier cities include Beijing, Guangzhou, and Shanghai, places that have dozens of McDonald's restaurants scattered throughout. Third-tier cities like Zhenjiang are much smaller, with maybe only one or two McDonald's restaurants alongside a slew of knockoffs.

I give up trying to find a signal and wave down a taxicab. The driver eagerly asks: "Guess you had to take a cab, not a DiDi, right? No cell phone service?" He explains that there's a serious protest in Zhenjiang today. Thousands of People's Liberation Army veterans have arrived from all parts of China, staging a massive protest by marching on the main city square. In response, the government shut down cell phone service in the downtown area, hoping to keep photos off social media and WeChat.

"What are they protesting about?" I ask. "Pensions," the taxi driver answers, and I see his grimace reflected in the rearview mirror. "What kind of society are we turning into," he says, "where we don't even give old army vets their pensions?"

I nod in agreement and we both fall silent, neither of us wanting to continue on the topic. In Xi Jinping's China, it's uncomfortable for two strangers to go too deep into the subject of *zhengzhi* (politics, 政治). There are no clear-cut consequences for discussing politics—after all, this is precisely how the system of censorship works, with a shadowy unease that looms over public conversations. Censorship is not made explicit; you just censor yourself. No one knows the consequences of critique, but no one wants to find out.

The Zhenjiang Vinegar Culture Museum is bustling today, and the guided tour I am on is full. The museum is located next to the Hengshun vinegar company's main factory, and pungent smells of fermentation waft through the building. Several college students are here, enjoying an outing without authority figures. A bored teenager is accompanied by her parents—when I ask where they are coming from, her parents tell me Nanjing, and that this is a celebratory post-*gaokao* trip. The *gaokao* is China's grueling university-entry test that spans three days, as the entire nation waits with anticipation for the average score. The nation's obsession with *gaokao* is similar to an academic March Madness. During *gaokao* week, weather and map apps on your phone will text to alert you: "It's raining, don't forget your umbrella on the way to the *gaokao*!" or "It's *gaokao* season, don't forget to be quiet and courteous! Valuing education and the future of our children are our socialist values!"

The tour meanders through a section on the historical vinegar-making process, where a large sign boasts VINEGAR TECHNOLOGY. Images printed on foam core of jet-black vinegar in bowls are mounted on the walls. Traditional Chinese vinegar is an inky substance that is both fragrant and sour.

At many tourist locations in China, tour guides and exhibits like to remind you that China was *the first*. The first in what? Well, just about anything. The first to invent gunpowder or paper, or to build a crazy-long wall . . . and vinegar is no exception. According to one panel, making vinegar was part of the *Qimin Yaoshu*, or Essential Techniques for the Welfare of the People, written 1,500 years ago, back when Europe was still in the Dark Ages. This was the text Charles Darwin referred to in studies on evolution, due to the *Qimin Yaoshu*'s references to breeding and animal domestication, reaffirming that the Chinese were *the first* to notice how genetic variation works.

The tour concludes in a mirrored hall with hundreds of vinegars on the shelf, from Heinz white vinegar to different types of balsamic. The tour guide cheerily describes it as a pleasant global vinegar showcase. She solemnly points out the packaging on genuine Hengshun Zhenjiang vinegar.

"And of course," she says, "you can always tell when a bottle is a fake. Fake vinegar is not fermented, so when you shake it, it will not foam up." Holding a bottle of real vinegar in one hand and a bottle of fake vinegar in the other, she briskly shakes both at the same time. "See?" she says. "See the difference?"

2.

Matilda Ho, founder of Bits x Bites, shakes my hand firmly and has precisely thirty minutes to talk. She has carefully drawn eyeliner and is carrying a MacBook Air in one arm. She speaks rapidly. Our conversation on food security and food safety unfolds over these thirty minutes at the Bits x Bites office in Shanghai, with a glass door so clean and transparent that I walked into it on my way to meet her.

Founded in China, Bits x Bites is the world's *first* venture capital fund dedicated to food innovation. Its mission is to "shape the future of good food," providing both investment returns and social benefit. The portfolio of Bits x Bites companies ranges from meal kits to lab-grown meat to "weather-proof farms" that provide a hermetic seal against the outside world of climate change; it also includes some gene-editing startups. In addition to Bits x Bites, Matilda is also the founder of Yimishiji, an online organic farmers market focused on the Shanghai-area "foodshed," a term used to describe the geographic area that grows and transports food for a particular population. A small village that relies on subsistence farming has a tiny, local foodshed, while certain upper-class consumers in Shanghai have a global foodshed.

The Yimishiji app is filled with images of beautiful produce. Sunlit eggs, streamlined stalks of celery, a lone bright orange carrot that seems to say demurely, *I am luxury, you want me.* Compared to the chaotic, open-air wet markets that most of China has traditionally shopped at, filled with slabs of fresh meat dangling on hooks, tanks of live seafood, and colossal piles of produce sold under tents, Yimishiji is a sharp break, catering to China's up-and-coming urban middle class. And unlike the food at China's open-air markets, all the items on Yimishiji have been independently tested for food safety. On Yimishiji, there are no bottles of fake vinegar. There are not even mass-produced products like Hengshun Zhenjiang vinegar.

Fake vinegar is the least of China's food-safety woes. A deliberately tongue-in-cheek headline from the Hong Kong newspaper *South China Morning Post* reads: FIRM USES HUMAN HAIR IN SOY SAUCE "BREAKTHROUGH." The article reveals that ground-up human hair was being put in soy sauce, cutting production costs by half. Profiteers diluted the original sauce with hair, then put the doctored soy sauce back in empty brand-name bottles and onto supermarket shelves.

Other unsavory cost-cutting techniques include making tapioca bubble tea balls with plastic green peas and using inedible red dyes on chilies. "Gutter oil," a type of recycled oil, is rampant, since cooking oil is a big expense, given the stir-fried nature of Chinese cuisine. Gutter oil entrepreneurs collect the massive amount of restaurant waste that is produced by millions of people eating out every night. They then filter and extract the oil back out of the waste, reselling the recycled oil to restaurants and supermarkets.

Food-safety incidents can be fatal. In 2008, before the Beijing Olympics, several infants in China died from kidney stones, and thousands more were suddenly sick, in critical condition. Investigators quickly traced the cause back to infant formula produced by Sanlu, a dairy company. The formula had been mixed with melamine. Melamine is similar in appearance to milk and boosts protein content. Often used in cattle feed, it is toxic to humans above certain doses. In order to increase profits and yield, farmers producing dairy for Sanlu had added melamine to their milk. The amount of melamine in Sanlu's infant formula exceeded the United Nations' food standard threshold for melamine in infant formula, with lethal results.

Existing food-safety scandals were just a small drop in a sea of risk. Matilda knows this all too well, with her background as a management consultant to multinational food corporations in China. As China's middle-class numbers increase to nearly half a billion, more of the world's population is demanding increased food choice and availability. Matilda points out that this is not a China-specific problem: middle-class consumers globally expect constant availability of a range of foods, and this lengthens the supply chain across towns, provinces, and countries, making it possible to always have strawberries at the supermarket, no matter what season it is. But with the addition of each block on the chain comes another potential source of failure.

Careful sourcing from farms is only part of the solution. Even the best products can be stymied by broken links in the cold chain during transport. Matilda gives the example of truck drivers, who will often turn off their refrigeration in order to save gasoline money and pocket the extra cash. When you start transporting food across hundreds of kilometers, control over the transportation process decreases. And due to effects on the ultimate food safety of perishable goods, this means, for consumers, the difference between a night out on the town and a night at the hospital.

3.

Traveling back from Shanghai, I talk to the political scientist and food-safety expert John Yasuda on the phone. He's in Oxford, England, and I'm standing on the second floor of the Shanghai Hongqiao train station, huddled in a McDonald's, one of the few quiet spots in the sprawling building. "Food safety is a nasty problem that combines macro-political, economic questions into a problem that is lived out day-to-day," John tells me. The more we talk, the more insurmountable food safety seems to become, given the interconnected, global span of the issue—a "wicked problem," a new type of problem whose name Horst Rittel and Melvin Webber coined to describe the increasingly entangled, global nature of related challenges.

Food safety is crucial for political stability, and is ultimately a reflection on a country's governance. For a long time, China's food woes were exacerbated by political corruption and bribery. In 2013, Xi Jinping made it a priority to address agriculture and food safety in China, remarking, "If our party can't even handle food-safety issues properly, then people will ask whether we are fit to keep ruling China."

The party's priority on food safety for political stability is manifested in its censorship of food-safety scandals.[1] After all, the numbers would cause government officials to lose face, undermining their authority. Compared to countries like Mexico and Turkey, which have similar GDPs per capita, China's food-safety index rating is significantly lower. Compared to countries like Singapore, with similarly authoritarian governments, China's food-safety score is shockingly low.

Why is China so bad at food safety? John elaborates on the problems of scale that Matilda mentioned. Feeding 22 percent of the world's population on 7 percent of the world's arable land is just plain difficult. Complicating this task are the demands on China's smallholder farmers. Nearly 98 percent of Chinese farmers have land that is less than the size of two football fields. There is enormous pressure on these farmers to produce enough food for the nation, ensuring food security. "The food bowl of the Chinese people must always remain firmly in their own hands,"[2] remarked Xi Jinping during his first few months as president in 2013. These farmers have additional pressure to produce enough food for export, which comprises 10 percent of China's massive GDP, alongside humanitarian relief food, crucial to China's bid as a global leader. And despite the amount of control the national government appears to have, the governance of food safety in China is fairly decentralized, with the bulk of the responsibility on province- and county-level agricultural bureaus.

Although centralization and consolidation seem like they might be the answer, industrialized agriculture would only displace farmers. As John points out, land in China is a precious resource, especially as China urbanizes and threatens the red line, an agricultural "defense line." Most of all, the land allocated to farmers serves as a basic form of poverty alleviation—no matter how poor you are, you can always go back to the land and farm food for yourself and your family. Privatizing land would only reproduce social inequality, John says, and that would threaten political stability.

Ultimately, food safety revolves around social trust, and John thinks that "social trust can't scale." When supply chains were shorter, being able to meet your farmer created this trust. With supply chains now long and complex, the chance you might meet the Australian farmer who grew the kiwi you eat or the Mexican farmer who produced the avocado on your plate is low. Farmers themselves are also isolated from seeing the people they provide food for; they send their products off to larger corporations that then redistribute them. These corporations demand low prices, squeezing farmers into a bind. In the case of Sanlu's melamine scandal, farmers felt the pressure from Sanlu to stretch their product to the point where it became lethal. This pressure to keep prices low increases with scale: the difference of a penny means a lot more when it's multiplied by millions of gallons of milk.

As John says this, I think of a common refrain I hear in China: "The West doesn't understand our problems. We just have too many people. The government has to operate at a scale you can't even imagine."

Staring out over the Shanghai Hongqiao train station, I watch as crowds of people line up, pushing each other through ticket gates, for sold-out high-speed trains that leave every five minutes. I wonder if it's all actually true.

That's the thing about trust. We live in a time when, through networks built using technology, there are more connections in the world. Can trust be easily extended? In the past, your network was small; you ate food produced by your local foodshed. Now, in cities, you rely on a much bigger network to put food on your plate.

In this light, the age-old argument for government can seem appealing: some kind of structure has to exist to mediate trust, to control the masses, the workers and farmers. The Chinese government is continuing its battle for food safety, with the same opacity it has always operated under. It's pursuing a variety of tactics, from increased involvement at the local level to using high-tech measures like blockchain in the newly formed Food Safety Cloud (食品安全云), to prevent record falsification at all points in the chain, whether at the local or the provincial scale.[3] The question is, will a large, lumbering government truly manage to help scale up social trust, given the mistrust people have toward the government already, after all the food-safety scandals? And if these initiatives operate as closed systems between the government and the corporations that make this technology, how can they regain the public's trust?

4.

On a humid summer day in the city of Guangzhou, I head to Alibaba's brand-new Hema supermarket with my uncle. Outside the supermarket is Hema's mascot, a giant hippopotamus in Alibaba blue. Its rotund snout takes up most of its face, leading to some peach emoji jokes online.

Hema supermarket is clean and precise, an off-line version of Yimishiji but with distinct differences: unlike the seasonal, local, organic foods that Yimishiji has, Hema has a vast selection of foods from any season, from any part of the world. Vacuum-sealed slabs of Norwegian farmed salmon from a special Alibaba–Norwegian Seafood Council partnership, raspberries from the United States, hunks of pork from Fujian, cherries from New Zealand, and soup dumplings from Shanghai all sit neatly under soothing lighting. All the food at Hema is guaranteed to be fresh, high quality, and most of all safe.

Shopping at Hema is not cheap, but that's what Alibaba and other tech companies are betting on. Over the past few years, tech companies including Alibaba, JD.com, and NetEase are all making forays into the food and food-retailing space, leveraging tight control over all degrees of the chain. These companies are centralizing production *and* shipping, with the help of informatics and sensors, giving consumers a sense of control over their food. This becomes apparent throughout the Hema store, as the prepackaged produce states the day of the week it was received in-store and the exact farm it came from.

As we wander through the aisles, my uncle stops in the seafood section. Seafood is a luxury in China, a luxury that more and more people can now afford. Live fish in tanks, paddling shrimp, and lobsters lumbering in crowded bins sit in the section, like a zoo exhibit. Chinese cuisine and eating habits demand fresh seafood, never frozen, killed the day of cooking.

Rather than trusting the government, people have shifted their trust to the private sector: Hema, Alibaba. This leads to cascading, glaring contradictions. The problems of food safety are the result of a privatized, free market model of agriculture with global reach—where competitive market behavior drives cost cutting. The government serves as a way to mediate social trust, to regulate and protect its citizens. Along the way, the government has struggled to be effective, which has conveniently led private companies to compete in the free market for a monopoly on food safety. Business articles laud Hema and other tech-company supermarkets as innovators digging into food safety: the same set of market forces that created the problem is now purportedly coming to the rescue.

For tonight, my aunt has requested we pick up several pounds of live shrimp. A few of them are at one end of the tank, reminding me of an aquarium display. Most are in the center, zooming around. My uncle sticks a net into the water, and some manage to flee. He pours dozens of swimming, frenzied shrimp into a big plastic bag, and places it in our cart. I stare as they dart back and forth, knocking into each other, beady black eyes protruding on stalks from the sides of their body. At this scale, a mass of shrimp seems more like a sinister invasion of insects than a tempting dinner.

5.

Chongqing is a sprawling, messy, mountainous city. The day I arrive, the air pollution is so thick it has blotted out the sun, casting a haze that turns the sky orange with a hint of gray. It looks like an apocalyptic-movie scene, as if the next rainstorm might topple the city. The "horizontal skyscraper" by the architect Moshe Safdie is almost finished. It's a long building that sits perilously atop three other skyscrapers, spanning several city blocks.

Through tunnels and over highways perched on mountains, my bus travels to Nanchuan District, two hours from the center of Chongqing. Another two hours and Chongqing's haze has been left behind. The bus goes through newly constructed tunnels, lights fresh and bright, untarnished, no buildup of dust from exhaust fumes.

I arrive in Sanqiao village, in the green mountains of Guizhou, where the blockchain chicken roams.

The village has a single paved road. The bus stop is next to a small store, and faces a large hill. I ask several people who are walking along the single road for directions to the village government headquarters. Sometimes the person does not understand me and I cannot understand them. In China's vast geography, each region has its own unique spoken dialect. Dialects can be so strong that fluent Mandarin speakers from elsewhere will not understand what a local person is saying. I can recall one visit to my mother's ancestral home when a cousin had to translate for me throughout the entire dinner.

This area of Guizhou has its own dialect as well as its own distinct language, given that it is home to the Miao ethnic minority. It's also one of the poorest regions in China, with an average household income of RMB 5,000 (about US$700) a year.

Sanqiao is dreamlike, with mountains covered in fog. I walk along a river with a small white bridge spanning a steep ravine. The village government headquarters stands on another daunting hill, past a battered-looking elementary school painted pink. I can hear the high pitch of children's voices reciting a poem.

A large red sign across from the newly constructed hospital reads BEING LAZY IS A DISGRACE, BEING SELF-RELIANT LEADS TO STRENGTH (好吃懒惰不光彩, 自力更生才出彩). It's one of the many political slogans that are part of the government's poverty-alleviation policy, and eerily reminiscent of several American values: Don't be lazy. Pull yourself up by the bootstraps. Hustle hard. Underneath the large red sign is a woman at a desolate fruit stand rearranging the oranges in her crate over and over. Hustle has come to Sanqiao.

6.

Blockchain chicken is not the actual name of the chicken I am here to see. The official name is Bubuji (步步鸡), or GoGoChicken, as some English PR materials call it. The COO of Shanghai Lianmo Technology, the company behind blockchain chicken, says that he explicitly keeps "blockchain" out of the name. To him, overhyped blockchain projects have turned the term "blockchain" into marketing gloss.

These blockchain chickens sell for up to RMB 300 (US$40) on JD.com. Typical buyers are upper-class urbanites—people willing to pay a premium on food.

I meet with one of the village secretary's fresh-faced assistants, Ren. He grew up in the county. He's thirty years old, and unlike many of his peers, he returned home after college in Chongqing, to help his ailing parents. He joined the local government because he figured if he had to come home, he might as well try to make the place he lived in a little less impoverished, a little more wealthy, and ultimately a little more lively.

We head to the GoGoChicken farm. As meat consumption increases in China, even places like KFC and McDonald's are subject to food-safety issues. Enter blockchain, the exotic technology that will address tracking and provenance, especially in chickens.

Ren tells me that, funnily enough, there've been a lot of GoGoChicken stories in the news, but very few visits to the farm. When we do get to the farm, I'm surprised by how friendly it looks. The entrance is small and peaceful, with brightly painted cartoon chickens on the walls.

Farmer Jiang is in charge of this blockchain chicken operation. He's wearing a straw hat in the rain. Behind him is a colorful mural of a chicken farmer with the same straw hat and chickens clustered around him. He's just plain nice.

Farmer Jiang has been raising chickens for a long time, long before blockchain was a technology. His specialty has always been *linxiaji* (under-the-tree chickens, 林夏季). They are free-range, vegetarian-fed chickens, the kind that roam around Sanqiao's lush canopy, getting plenty of exercise. Typical overstuffed chickens on industrial poultry farms are fed constantly in order to reach the correct weight for slaughter in under one month. These free-range blockchain chickens are raised for at least three months before slaughter. As Farmer Jiang describes the chickens' diet of local corn, my mouth starts watering at how delicious their eggs must be.

The GoGoChicken project is a partnership between the village government and Lianmo Technology, a company that applies blockchain to physical objects, with a focus on provenance use cases—that is, tracking where something originates from. When falsified records and sprawling supply chains lead to issues of contamination and food safety, blockchain seems like a clear, logical solution.

That is one of the many promises of blockchain. In its origins, blockchain was structured with a set of assumptions about the social conditions under which it operates, and many of its advocates and engineers have pushed a political vision of the world that is somewhere between libertarianism and anarchy. But like a lot of technology these days, it has been adopted by companies and governments to make money, including a chicken farm in a small remote village of Guizhou.

Farmer Jiang says that raising free-range chickens is a yearly uphill battle. One set of problems was the threat of disease, and the material difficulties of making sure several thousand chickens survived over three months.

"Chickens aren't very smart," Farmer Jiang says as we walk around the farm, into a neatly kept feeding barn. "Or brave. If you have them outside of cages, at night they can get scared. They cluster around lights and they overcrowd each other, killing each other. A kind of chicken stampede."

The bigger problem was that Jiang didn't have a reliable market every year. He had to do all the selling and marketing himself. Even when he did make a sale, the profit margin was low or he sold at a loss. Buyers had a difficult time trusting him, and trusting that the chickens were indeed free-range, worth the higher asking price.

Then Zhou Ling arrived from Shanghai, to serve as the Sanqiao village aid cadre. China's poverty-alleviation efforts deploy millions of aid cadres across China, typically younger members of the party, who provide all kinds of assistance and relief, including repairing water pumps and conducting digital literacy initiatives. These poverty-alleviation programs reflect China's "fragmented authoritarianism," which is both decentralized and autocratic: decentralized at the local scale with fairly loose controls, but authoritarian on national policies.[4] The contradiction of this fragmented-authoritarian model can create a lot of confusion between the official policy and what is actually happening on the ground.

Zhou connected Farmer Jiang with Lianmo Technology, which was hoping to pilot more blockchain and Internet of Things projects, including the profitable business of poultry tracking, as China consumes five billion chickens a year (which is still only about half the American chicken-consumption rate of nine billion per year).

Jiang shows us around the rest of the farm—several pristine feeding areas, and the "control" room where the base station sits. Each chicken wears an ankle bracelet that is physically tamperproof, which tracks characteristics such as number of steps taken and the location of the chicken. A chicken Fitbit of sorts.

The front plate of the ankle bracelet has a QR code on it. All this data is viewable on a website accessible with a password, and the website includes constantly streaming surveillance footage of the chickens to ensure that they have not been adulterated in any way by an intruder. There's also a map of the chickens' movements. Data about the chickens is uploaded via the base station to Anlink, a proprietary enterprise blockchain that is an experiment by the sprawling ZhongAn, an online-only insurance company.

Sanqiao chickens are under heavy surveillance. In addition to wearing the ankle bracelets, the chickens are tested every two weeks by the local branch of the Ministry of Agriculture for any signs of antibiotic usage, which is illegal under the category of free-range. While it may seem like overkill, it might be a small price to pay in order to win back public trust.

These chickens are delivered to consumers' doors, butchered and vacuum sealed, with the ankle bracelet still attached, so customers can scan the QR code before preparing the chicken. Scanning this code leads them to a page with details about the chicken's life, including its weight, the number of steps it took, and its photograph. In Shanghai, these details are seen as a sign of authenticity and food safety, while in the United States they could easily be read from an animal-welfare angle. Farmer Jiang lets me scan an ankle bracelet, and the experience is underwhelming. While I know this is actual information about the chicken, it would be easy for Lianmo Technology to create a series of fake web pages for these chickens. Since the Anlink blockchain is an enterprise blockchain, consumers have little interaction with that part of the technology.

The village secretary's assistant, Ren, and I head back to Jiang's house for tea. It's a humble home with three rooms. In one corner of the living room is a stove with a large metal top—it functions as a table, stove, and hearth for Guizhou's chilly winters. Jiang's mother is there, along with his wife. A flat-screen TV is behind him—the product of blockchain chicken earnings from last year.

In the end, Jiang sold six thousand chickens through the blockchain project. And as part of the communal nature of village life, several other local families were employed by the project. In a poverty-alleviation effort, profits were redistributed between Farmer Jiang's family and the three hundred other households in the village.

Despite its success, the future of blockchain chicken

is uncertain. Neither the code, nor the equipment, nor the software belongs to Jiang: it ultimately remains Lianmo Technology's. Jiang tells me that last year, Lianmo Technology's GoGoChicken project ordered six thousand chickens in advance, to sell off to JD.com's online supermarket and other platforms. There was no such order this year, so Jiang is left on his own. Ren's boss, the village's party secretary, Chairman Chen, is currently in talks with a company to provide chickens to nearby Chongqing. As with a lot of startups, uncertainty swirls around how the technical infrastructure will continue to function, and whether Lianmo Technology will continue to support a project with such high overhead costs.

Farmer Jiang has more buyers for his free-range chickens now that they are blockchain free-range chickens. But in switching to blockchain, the farmer's overhead has increased significantly, with the cost of the ankle bracelets and the technical infrastructure. By the end of the process, Farmer Jiang makes RMB 100 (US$14) on each chicken, not accounting for costs.

Still, Jiang is optimistic. He's no longer a stranger to the process of raising surveilled chickens. With the slow influx of money to the village, a postsecondary vocational school is being built. Other projects like a "smart mushroom tent" have arrived, sponsored by the state-owned liquor company, Kweichow Moutai. The watering and the temperature and humidity of the tent are controlled automatically by a system of sensors, producing cremini and shiitake mushrooms on logs.

As we sit in his house, with our feet around the

hearth, Farmer Jiang starts gathering up oranges and putting them into a plastic bag. He admits that it's not easy for this area of Guizhou to develop economically. It's the geography, he says. It's remote, it's mountainous. The terrain makes it difficult to farm certain crops. But precisely because it is remote, it boasts a pollution-free environment, with fresh air and clean soil. The problem is, the villagers don't quite know how to put a dollar value on that. I tell him, I'm not sure anyone does.

As Ren and I leave, Farmer Jiang hands us the big plastic bag of oranges. "Take these! I grew these myself for my family! They're organically farmed. I used the GoGoChicken poop as fertilizer."

In the car, driving through the small mountain paths back to the bus stop, I ask Ren, "So, what do you think of *qukuailian* [blockchain, 区块链]?" Although we've seen the GoGoChicken farm, I haven't explicitly brought up blockchain at all during my visit.

"Blockchain? What's blockchain?" asks Ren.

7.

Onstage at the Internet Archive's Decentralized Web Summit in San Francisco, the founder of the Lightning Network, a protocol layer that sits on top of Bitcoin's blockchain, is speaking into the microphone. The Decentralized Web Summit is host to an eclectic assortment of people, a caricature of the Bay Area's tech scene.

The speaker is reed thin and bespectacled, and both of his hands firmly grasp the sides of the podium. His shoulders are slightly slouched. The audience sits rapt, eagerly waiting to hear what he has to say.

"Life is 'nasty, brutish, and short,' right?" He pauses, then talks about Usenet, a distributed message board system. He attributes the demise of Usenet to what he calls bad actors—essentially, jerks. He continues, "That's always been the problem with society. Society has always had the issue of assholes ruining it for everybody."

The sentiment he shares is common among cryptocurrency and blockchain enthusiasts—a cynical view of human nature, where people are selfish and untrustworthy. The idea that life is "nasty, brutish, and short" comes from the political and moral philosophy of Thomas Hobbes, who argued that a strong, authoritarian government is needed to curb the selfish instinct that lives in all of us. A few hundred years later, the "tragedy of the commons" concept would solidify Hobbes's thinking as scientific. Many crypto and blockchain enthusiasts will cite this concept often and candidly.

The concept of the tragedy of the commons was popularized in 1968 by the ecologist Garrett Hardin, who also argued that the overpopulation of the earth would lead to disaster because of finite resources. Hardin's tragedy of the commons was the condition where individual users, motivated by their own self-interest, ruin a shared resource system for everyone. Hardin gave the example of herders who, caring only about the survival of their own herds, destroyed pastures by overgrazing common land.

Like his theories on overpopulation, Hardin's tragedy of the commons was later exposed as deeply problematic, as politics disguised as science. His scientific ideas stemmed from his racist, eugenicist beliefs as a white nationalist, and many of the groups he saw as unable to manage shared resources were in non-Western countries.[5]

And setting aside Hardin's political ideologies, the tragedy of the commons theory is just plain wrong. The concept was disproved with in-depth data and careful science in 1990 by Elinor Ostrom, who would be awarded a Nobel Prize for her work.

However, since Hardin was an ecologist, the tragedy of the commons became naturalized, seen as neutral science rather than political belief. In reality, Hardin's ideas were based on terrifying assumptions, a world in which human nature and natural resources were static, finite, and fixed.

Despite Ostrom's work, the belief in innate human selfishness in a world of scarcity had become ingrained outside of ecology—in fields like information science and economics.[6] This belief in selfishness and scarcity is one of the core ideologies that gave rise to blockchain.

Although blockchain has become synonymous with Bitcoin, they are not quite the same. Bitcoin is one use of blockchain, but it remains separate from blockchain technology. Some have used a biological analogy to illustrate the difference: if blockchain is DNA, Bitcoin is a distinct species. Blockchain is a special kind of distributed record-keeping system that uses cryptography to prevent records from being falsified, eliminating the need to trust a centralized authority to verify records.

For example, since food-safety inspection records in China are subject to falsification, instead of there being one canonical record owned by one organization that could be tampered with, a number of records could exist. These records could be distributed among many people: the farmer, the local inspection bureau, the end consumer. If these records are coordinated and kept in sync through a system, people could trust this distributed system rather than a central government authority to deem food safe. If one bad actor at the local inspection bureau did try to fudge the register, the system would reject the change, making it nearly impossible to falsify a record. The special thing about this system is that the distributed record keepers wouldn't have to trust one another; they may never even have to interact with each other, instead letting the technology mediate. This system of coordination and enforcement is blockchain—immutable, tamperproof records that have a range of mechanisms built in to prevent bad actors. To me, this system sounds ideal at first blush. But the technical implementation of such a system creates a different reality.

In blockchain, a set of records is called a block. Multiple computers, or nodes, hold a list of prior records. Each block of records is mathematically chained to the previous block of records. In order to link the blocks, a "hashing function" has to be performed by computers: guessing random numbers to solve a math problem, a task that requires enormous amounts of computing power and electricity.

After this hashing function, blocks are then on the blockchain, and this is transmitted to all the other computers on the network. Since the blocks are all mathematically chained together, to falsify a record would mean having to redo all the work for subsequent blocks on the chain, requiring so much electricity and resources that falsification is disincentivized.

Bitcoin arrived in 2008, at the beginning of a global financial crisis. At the time, a paper was circulated online, written by someone named Satoshi Nakamoto, proposing a peer-to-peer currency. The paper outlined this peer-to-peer currency, or Bitcoin, as Nakamoto called it. Instead of a central bank verifying transactions and preventing double spending, Nakamoto proposed the system of blockchain to verify and keep records of transactions. Bitcoin would be the incentive for people with computers to verify and put blocks on the blockchain. This is the core of the Bitcoin blockchain. It leads with the idea that bad actors are intrinsic in a system, and to prevent their actions, enormous amounts of electricity must be spent on preventing them through hashing functions.

The first block on the Bitcoin blockchain was created along with the text "THE TIMES 03/JAN/2009 Chancellor on brink of second bailout for banks"—the anti-centralization message of Bitcoin coming through loud and clear. And since 2008, the cryptocurrency and blockchain space has blossomed beyond Bitcoin into other currencies and other blockchains, currencies like Ethereum and EOS, all with slightly different consensus algorithms—ways of ensuring that individual computers, or nodes, have records that agree with each other.

Hardin's original essay in 1968 used the example of the medieval commons, a place where peasants grazed their cows. According to Hardin, the ungoverned nature of the commons led to overgrazing, which is why the commons had to eventually be enclosed and privatized. Yet Hardin was also wrong about this history—the commons model had actually thrived in Europe for hundreds of years. The mismanagement of the commons by peasants was a lie, an excuse made up by powerful landowners who wanted to seize and control these spaces.

During a long conversation with a Chinese blockchain engineer, I learn that the core belief of a government like China's is steeped in what is termed "patriarchal authoritarianism": its citizens cannot be trusted, so the government needs to control them. Citizens must trust that the predominantly male-led government has their best interests at heart. The government expects its citizens to believe that the system works, without question, by instilling fear that without it a few bad actors would ruin things for everyone. And so the story of blockchain in China seems like a game of pick your poison: Who do you trust more, the machine or the government?

Blockchain, like an authoritarian regime, uses a parallel logic: people cannot be trusted in a free market, and bad actors are intrinsic to a social system. In order to mediate trust, a technical infrastructure is better than a government; governments are made up of fallible people, whereas technical infrastructure works automatically. Instead of the government moderating trust, blockchain does so with machines.

At the Decentralized Web Summit, I attend a few technical sessions, rooms filled with blockchain developers who hold an enormous amount of power through the technical decisions they make. In the blockchain space, technical problems and challenges are intrinsically linked to governance issues. For example, certain vulnerabilities within blockchains in the past have led to further technical decisions, decisions that have threatened the idea that blockchain should be immutable in the first place. Code and law become conflated in the blockchain.

And that leads to a widespread belief that the blockchain should be governed by the community of developers around it. In recent years, the community has become increasingly well funded by venture capital, with millions of dollars being doled out to blockchain projects that only further solidify the political system we live in. When I look around at the community present at the conference, most of the developers are white and male. This community does not include people like Ren and Jiang. One speaker at the conference, Karissa McKelvey of Digital Democracy, puts it, "Blockchain governance is not unbiased or neutral. It's just shifting bureaucratic roles to more technical roles. At some point, you have to trust someone." Given the demographics of those in the technical roles, McKelvey bluntly says, "You might even say it's colonialism."

A system of record keeping used to be textual, readable,

and understandable to everyone. The technical component behind it was as simple as paper and pencil. That system was prone to falsification, but it was widely legible. Under governance by blockchain, records are tamperproof, but the technical systems are legible only to a select few. Even exploring transactions on a blockchain requires some amount of technical knowledge and access. The technology of record keeping has become increasingly more complex. This complexity requires trust and faith in the code—and trust in those who write it. For those of us who don't understand the code, trusting a record written in natural language on a piece of paper seems at the very least a lot clearer.

We trust all sorts of technical systems every day without having to read their code. The software that flies our planes, runs our city trains. Like a lot of emerging technologies, blockchain is beholden only to its makers, and to a handful of well-funded companies. The conventional answer to this is to suggest government regulation of software, as is the case with airplane and train software. Yet the political ethos of blockchain is precisely about taking power away from a central authority like the government. And deep down, I find that sentiment admirable. However, blockchain has yet to answer the question: If it takes power away from a central authority, can it truly put power back in the hands of the people, and not just a select group of people? Will it serve as an infrastructure that amplifies trust, rather than increasing both mistrust and a singular reliance on technical infrastructure? Will it provide ways to materially organize and enrich a community, rather than further accelerating financial systems that serve a select few? Can the community expand and diversify itself, so that it does not reproduce the system of power and patriarchy that it is attempting to dismantle?

I wander through the Decentralized Web Summit, sipping a grapefruit LaCroix and peering into rooms illuminated by neon lights. Years ago, I would have gotten an enormous thrill from this conference: the light-filled rooms, the eccentric but well-dressed audience who jet around from Berlin to San Francisco with casual, glittering affluence, after-parties with good drugs at plush lofts, and most of all, the way changing the world seems to be just a keystroke away. A few people here are "blockchain bros," young men hyped on internet culture and the promise of blockchain. Some of them are ready to pitch their companies at any given moment. More recently, popular support for Bitcoin and cryptocurrency has oscillated between feverish excitement and wariness about its electricity consumption—it requires more electricity annually than Switzerland. By creating a system based on the assumption that humans are destructive and selfish, you only end up making those assumptions reality: a self-fulfilling prophecy. It serves as a reminder of the physical, material relationships that bind our world together.

There is some debate about whether blockchain and crypto are here to stay, whether the technology is actually able to do all the things it says it will do. I think of the melamine-milk scandal, and whether blockchain would have helped in that situation. The contamination came from farmers, driven by economic pressures. Blockchain wouldn't have helped prevent falsification, but it would have made the milk more expensive. Under authoritarianism, which benefits from holding expertise within its realm of power, and under an economic system that thrives off inequality in creating a market, of course blockchain is here to stay. It creates another layer of inequality, another incentive to make food a commodity.

That is the intrinsic flaw, the infuriating circular logic. We operate under game theory conditions, under market forces, under the belief that we *will* lie to each other because someone else has more, and we have more to gain. And so we create solutions that further exacerbate this inequality. This is what happens when resources like food are treated as commodities to be bought and sold, to make money from, instead of as a basic human right.

In some of the projects being discussed in rooms at the Decentralized Web Summit, the utopian language makes me cringe. Other projects give me significantly more hope. A decentralized web does not necessarily mean blockchain; it can include other tools that promote shared, community management in a legible way. These projects, many of which are alternatives to blockchain, feel exciting, almost utopian.

The truth is, we all want some kind of utopia, even if utopia is, by definition, not a place. We want a way for things to get better, to get perfect. What many of us are feeling right now, what we see, is that the existing economic systems don't serve us.

As I run into friends at the conference and we discuss the talks we've attended, I know that I too want things to get better, and that I hold hope for technology to help us fix things—I remain, in some ways, an unabashed techno-optimist.

During lunch, I sit in a sunlit room, eating a chicken sandwich. This is where my travels get weird. For all our models of what will happen in a decentralized age, for all our incredible new technologies, we still cling to fictions about human nature. We have sequenced the human genome and we believe that humans can evolve, become ever more advanced. Yet, instead of designing technology that fosters and cultivates communal behaviors of trust, we still design technology that assumes scarcity and cultivates selfishness. This coercive design relies on a view of human nature that comes from a Hobbesian era when people barely had running water, a fictional, universal view of humanity that has been disproved over and over by research.

I think back to a different lunch, to my lunch with Ren before I visited the blockchain chicken farm. It was, ironically, a vegetarian meal at a small restaurant in the village. A large digital clock with the printed words COMPUTER ETERNITY TIME hung above us, red LCD numbers changing every minute as if it were showing an inevitable count toward fictional progress. I wonder: Who must agree to live in fictions that someone else wrote, and who has the power to write fictions for the rest of us? And if anyone can write fictions, why can't we write new ones?

.3.

When AI Farms Pigs

1.

It is November 2018. In the city of Guangzhou, African swine fever still feels distant. I'm in the city visiting my aunt and uncle, enjoying the swimming pool in their luxury apartment complex and loading up on imported Australian trail mix before I head back to the countryside. Along the balconies of people's high-rise apartments are slabs of meat, tied with string. The slabs sway next to shirts and sheets left out to dry. Late autumn means it's time to make *lap yuk*, preserved pork, a southern Chinese specialty. A piece of raw pork belly is soaked in a blend of rice wine, salt, soy sauce, and spices, then hung out to cure in the damp, cold autumn air. The fat becomes translucent and imparts a savory-sweet taste to any stir-fried vegetable dish. A relative of mine explains that only southern China can make preserved pork like this. The secret is the native, natural spores and bacteria in the wind.

I wake up every day at 5:00 a.m. and read Pig Progress, a popular pork industry news source. There is a global pig panic and a pig lockdown in rural China, born out of biosecurity and the onset of African swine fever (ASF), a disease in pigs that causes hemorrhaging. The fatality rate is close to 100 percent, as pigs bleed out to their deaths. Headlines in my news feed declare a world on edge. While ASF has been in other countries, such as Russia and Belgium, this is the first time the fever has been reported in China, the world's largest pork producer. The looming impacts are an unpleasant prospect for economists and politicians. Less pork available means higher food prices, and higher food prices means public discontent. Historical lessons abound: bread riots have been catalysts for the demise of empires, from the French Revolution to the Russian February Revolution. No one wants a pork riot.

Pork dishes are a large part of Han Chinese cuisine. Pigs were domesticated in China as far back as 7000 B.C.E., and a 1929 anthropological survey showed that 70 percent of animal calorie intake in China was from pork. Within traditional Chinese medicine, food itself is medicine, and is crucial to the prevention of disease. Pork nourishes the blood and strengthens qi, the vital life force that flows through all living beings. Dishes are expected to be a balance of all five flavors, for medicinal benefit—sweet, salty, bitter, spicy, sour. Mao Zedong's favorite dish, red braised pork, adheres to this flavor criteria, with the addition of extra chilies that signal the spiciness and revolutionary zeal of Mao's native Hunan Province.

While pork was once an occasional luxury, incomes and pork consumption are rising across China. This increased appetite is shifting geopolitical alliances and global trade. In 2013, the Henan Province–based WH Group bought the American pork producer Smithfield, making the WH Group the largest pork producer in the world. It expanded WH Group's operations to a vast network of family farms and industrial operations outside of China. These industrial pig farms are an environmental headache for the communities that live around them, including states like North Carolina, which has launched legislative campaigns against Smithfield. In 2005, Brazil's minister of foreign relations remarked on the rosy Brazil-China relationship as being part of the "reconfiguration of the world's commercial and diplomatic geography." Brazil is poised to be the world's leader in soybean exports as swaths of the Amazon rain forest are deforested for soy farming. Eighty percent of the harvest ends up as pig feed, and China is currently the top buyer of Brazilian soy.

Countries like the United States have wheat reserves as insurance against famine, and to control food prices. China is the only country in the world to have a pork reserve, consisting of millions of live pigs and uncountable pounds of frozen pork, hoarded from domestic and foreign sources. When the country experienced a 2008 food price surge, the government drew upon these pork reserves, which is how Smithfield pork ended up in China en masse.

In Xiangyang village, a few hours outside of Guangzhou, I eat preserved pork for breakfast, lunch, and dinner. I've been back in China for a few weeks now and pigs have become elusive. Unlike in previous years, when the aggressive snorting of pigs seemed to be present in most villages I walked through, autumn has turned into winter and pigs are nowhere to be found. Paranoia over ASF has led the local government to preventatively mass slaughter pigs that reside in small-scale family operations, reasoning that small farmers are unable to keep to biosecurity measures as tightly as industrial operations. I'm supposed to be researching pig farming in the countryside, but the animal is nowhere to be found.

I annoy my host in Xiangyang with a slew of questions. "Do you raise pigs in the village? Where does this preserved pork come from? How much do you pay for pork? How do you raise pigs?" My host is incredulous at the simplemindedness of my questions. "Why would we raise pigs here?" he responds. "Pigs are so hard to raise well," he tells me. "They're smart animals and have a lot of needs. When you feed them, you have to buy grain, and then cook the grain, since they won't eat it raw. They're like humans. Even then, when you sell the pork, you'd never make back the money you invested in feed. Pork sells for cheap at markets these days; you can't just go selling expensive pork and expect people to buy it."

He pauses. "We used to raise pigs in the village. They help our farming. You can use their waste for fertilizer. But then we finally got this paved road that connects the village to the rest of the county. People come around twice a week in cars, selling us pork, including the preserved pork you're eating. It's so much cheaper to buy pork than to raise your own. You'd be an idiot to raise your own."

Through friends, I manage to get in contact with just such an idiot named Li Jianhu, who runs an ecological pork CSA (community-supported agriculture) operation in Fujian. He's plugged into the small-scale organic pork farming scene in southern China, so I'm hoping he can help me find a pig farm to visit. He says he'll ask around, but no promises. Security is tight. African swine fever is serious.

Jianhu explains that the virus is typically spread from snout-to-snout contact in wild boars, but has now infected domesticated pigs. If a pig does manage to survive ASF, it carries the disease for the rest of its life. The current disease vector of ASF in domesticated pigs is entirely human made.

Instead of following the physical snout-to-snout models of disease transfer, which can be contained in one area, ASF is now spreading rapidly, jumping over several kilometers. It's a resilient, contagious virus, and can even be spread through meat, including processed meat products like sausages, surviving UV light and extreme temperatures. Customs officials at borders are all on high alert after one Chinese tourist arriving in Thailand was found to have a lone ASF-contaminated sausage in a carry-on.

Li Jianhu eventually gets back to me with no promising news. The situation is dire. He's had to shut down his own pork CSA, given the newly implemented, highly restrictive policies for transporting pigs from farm to slaughterhouse. Even the Shanghai Meishan Pig Species Protection Farm, a tourist farm that relies on throngs of visitors to survive, is now closed.

This is a big moment, Jianhu says. Prior to 2018, ASF had never entered China. The threat isn't just to China's pork supply but also to the world's. China exports all sorts of pork products, from blood-clotting heparin to the protein powders in our smoothies, and all of these products are potential vehicles for ASF. As of 2018, ASF had never been reported within the United States.

According to Jianhu, the first case of ASF in China was in a backyard pork operation, one of the many midsize pork farms with fewer than a hundred pigs. Ninety-eight percent of the pork farms in China have fewer than fifty animals, and these small to midsize farms account for about a third of pork production in China. These highly decentralized farms make government oversight difficult. There is also enormous pressure for these farms to keep up with the market price for pork, and to maintain steady production. The government was finding ASF a convenient excuse to eradicate these small farms, making way for centralized, industrial-scale operations.

Industrial scale is where things were headed anyway, says Li Jianhu. "Over the past ten years, big capital has entered the picture." Two-thirds of pork production is now concentrated in large corporations that are determined to do their patriotic duty: create China's pork miracle. Through cost cutting and technological magic, China would produce enough cheap pork to meet demand.

We created the ASF epidemic, says Jianhu, out of the quest for cheap pork. One of the ways to ensure cheap pork is to lower the cost of feeding pigs. Xiangyang village's pigs were fed cooked grains and beans fit for human consumption. ASF has been transferred through industrial pig swill.

Industrial pig swill is a finely tuned version of animal Soylent—a combination of GMO soybeans, grains, protein powders, and sometimes treated food waste. Treated food waste often contains pork, and the added protein powders are often derived from pigs. We are feeding pigs themselves.[1] Many of us are unable to see this operation—for example, in the United States, there are "ag-gag" laws that make it illegal to even photograph industrial feeding operations. It's in this opacity that industrial swill proliferates, keeping prices low. This swill is fully *optimized*: the optimal set of nutrients for a pig to grow to an appropriate size, to get to market in the optimal time. And so pigs unknowingly cannibalize each other, infecting and reinfecting their own kind.

"Even if you do get to an industrial pig farming operation, what would you do there?" Jianhu asks. It's not like I'd get to see any of the pigs close-up. In industrial pig farming, there is little contact between humans and pigs, and the pigs remain behind closed doors, viewable only on closed-circuit TV. Pigs have a fragile constitution. One pig farmer told me that pigs can get stressed and sick just from a minor change in their drinking water. Even under the best circumstances, without the threat of ASF, an industrial pig farm is more like an iPhone factory than a bucolic countryside haven. Each herd is watched and monitored on-screen for any signs of sickness or disease. When human intervention is required, people enter wearing disinfected hazmat suits and face masks, looking less like the blockchain chicken farmer Jiang and more like a worker inside a silicon chip factory.

2.

Right now, delicious, chef-lauded pork in China is being produced by NetEase, one of the world's largest, most profitable internet gaming companies. Ding Lei, the founder of NetEase, was eating hot pot with friends and began to worry that the blood tofu, a traditional hot pot ingredient made of coagulated pigs' blood, was fake. In this moment, Lei's business plans turned from gaming to pig farming.

Since 2009, in Lushan, Zhejiang, NetEase has been perfecting the art of raising pigs under Weiyang, its new agricultural products division.[2] The farm in Lushan has the precision of an electronics factory and the feeling of the world's most sterile, meticulous resort. On this farm, pigs live an optimized life, with an optimal amount of exercise and an optimal swill mix. They even listen to a soothing soundtrack, carefully designed for stress relief. This music is beneficial for us, as pork eaters. Stress before slaughter can alter a pig's metabolism, increasing cortisol and resulting in what's known in the industry as "DFD" (dark, firm, dry) meat. Weiyang pork is now available online and at special Weiyang retail stores scattered across China's software capital, Hangzhou.

More than a lone founder's quest for pork purity or sheer novelty, NetEase's foray into the food space is a clever business move. As Matilda mentioned to me in Shanghai, information about food is central to food safety. This makes industrialized farming, including modern pig farming, an information business, with a focus on scaling trust. NetEase Weiyang declares itself to be combining "internet thinking and modern agriculture." And part of internet thinking involves farming at a scale and degree of precision possible in software—a level of control over every microscopic variable along the way, such as pig stress levels. Weiyang's entire approach is crudely transparent—food, like engineers, can be a pipeline and sourcing issue, solved through increased vertical integration. NetEase has set up numerous massive online open courses (MOOCs) to create a population of skilled workers for recruiting directly into their company, addressing the existing shortage of skilled high-tech workers. Similarly, Weiyang skips the step of working with sources, instead creating its own source of high-quality pork, further eliminating any point of failure.

3.

On my way to visit the Alibaba headquarters in Hangzhou, I stop in the chaotic inland city of Guiyang, a tech boomtown that is building at a frenetic rate. Tencent, Alibaba, and Apple are all carving data centers into caves close to the city, hidden by subtropical trees. The entire city is an alien terrain—flat earth with mountains that seem to rise out of nowhere. Buildings hang off the sides of those mountains, with sky bridges connecting skyscrapers. Couriers on motorcycles weave around cars stuck in traffic. Drivers honk aggressively, with cigarettes dangling from their lips, windows rolled down. The scent of smog and smoke sticks to the back of my throat. Guiyang has a few nicknames. Locals call it mini Hong Kong for its vibrant, bacchanalian nightlife, but insist that Guiyang surpasses Hong Kong with its unique culture of constant, unabashed pleasure seeking—an ability to deal with worries tomorrow and enjoy life in the present.

It's evening and the sky is a dark orange as city lights cast a ghoulish veil in the haze of pollution. I leave the tiny efficiency studio I'm staying at, on the fortieth floor of a high-rise apartment building. The building brims with voices, with electronic dance music, with the sounds of living. The elevator stops at nearly every floor, a voyeuristic descent. Floor thirty-eight is a high-end hair salon, with two young women waiting in satin robes, tapping away at their cell phones. Floor thirty-five is dark, empty, a construction site filled with debris, old appliances, and a metal cot. A migrant worker dressed in dusty camouflage gets on the elevator, holding an empty plastic pail and a towel; he's likely sleeping on this floor during his construction-work stint. Floor thirty-three is a karaoke (KTV) club, illuminated pink with two women clad in white tops and denim miniskirts at reception. Floor thirteen is residential. A child drives onto the elevator in a red toy Mercedes, accompanied by his mother, a woman with bleached-blond hair. Each floor is mesmerizing, an intimate map of complicated lives, shaped by the uneven contours of this mountainous city.

When the elevator gets to the lobby, I walk through a set of glass doors past a sleeping security guard. Pig life is still on my mind. I wonder: Can life be optimized? And if it can, what would you even optimize for?

An entire industry of scientists, swine technicians, genetic testing companies, educational institutions, and industrial-farm managers exist in order to optimize porcine life. Corporations like the Pig Improvement Company harness computational genetics and cutting-edge biology to design pigs specifically for industrial farming. Increased agricultural automation has led to pigs becoming physically standardized, much like our fruits and vegetables. As with an assembly line in a factory, scaling from producing one hundred pigs to a hundred thousand means requiring parts to be the same size and type, interchangeable. Before the advent of industrial agriculture in China, farmers raised hundreds of pig breeds of different sizes and attributes. These pigs were adapted to local climates and diseases, providing a receptacle for leftovers and generating rich fertilizer for fields.

Industrial pig farming uses only a few breeds, such as the highly popular hybrid DLY (a cross between Duroc, Landrace, and Yorkshire). Even the unwanted attributes of these pigs are slowly being refined, edited out—physical traits like tails, which are a nuisance in transport, since in crowded conditions stressed piglets will bite each other's tails off. Combined with genetic control, automatic feeder and water-dispenser systems, and strict exercise times, pigs are farmed to precise size.

The hubris of optimizing life assumes levers of control: you can optimize for something if you think you know the outcome, if you've convinced yourself that you have managed to quantify all the variables. But in an uncertain, irrational world, nothing is guaranteed. The systems of industrial agriculture constantly seek to eliminate any uncertainty. For porcine life, levers of control exist from the small scale of pig DNA to the large infrastructural systems of slaughterhouses designed to decrease stress (and improve the texture of pork). As ASF unfolds in China, it's clear that optimization has wrought a complex system with consequences humans could never have imagined in our precise models and calculations. These consequences expose that sense of control as a total delusion. Yet the quest for optimization continues.

Our own lives are being threatened by this hubristic optimization process. The appearance of new human diseases such as bird flu and other novel influenzas like COVID-19—zoonotic diseases that cross from animal to human—coincide with our modern era of optimizing life, of industrialized agriculture and subsequent habitat loss. The evolutionary biologist Rob Wallace has shown how this highly optimized, industrial farming of meat is leading to the unchecked creation of devastating new pathogens. For multinational agribusinesses and the governments that support them, "it pays to produce a pathogen that could kill a billion people." A 2015 paper on zoonotic disease worriedly proclaims that 60 percent of all emerging diseases are now zoonotic, and 80 percent of new pathogens come from the top pork-producing countries—places like China.[3] With meat consumption growing worldwide, we might just eat enough to also snuff ourselves out.

Outside the apartment building in Guiyang, people are just starting to eat their second dinner at 10:00 p.m., a habit that I am told is intrinsic to hard-partying Guiyang. It's technically a Tuesday, but in Guiyang, every night feels like a Friday.

Street vendors and informal food stalls have sprung up along sidewalks, illuminated by glowing signs and incandescent bulbs drooping from extension cords. One vendor brings out bowls of steaming rice noodles in a salty broth, with trails of spicy red oil and ground pork, garnished with pickles and peanuts. Revelers sit on tiny stools surrounding low plastic tables. Trash piles into the storm drains in the street, a mess of skewers, noodles, and hot pot remnants. Dozens of empty bottles sit next to one table, as a group of middle-aged men slurp noodles and drink beer out of small, thin-walled plastic cups. They toast each other, they give toasts to good health. They drunkenly toast this evening, a precious sliver of time together, under the weight of their responsibilities and hardships. "At our age, it isn't easy to find time to be with each other, and we've all been through a lot to be here today," one of them says, voice slurring with emotion. I sit, eating alone. After traveling by myself for days on end, I watch with a tinge of jealousy as they relish this evening. A visceral glow of life surrounds them. In this glow, the word "commitment" surfaces. A commitment to the path of living as life unfolds, no matter how it transforms. A desire to keep living, not against but *with* the specter of frailty, failure, and death. This commitment is a naked pleasure that exists under the ever-shifting, open space of change, palpable against the hungry, narrow world of optimization. It would be impossible to optimize life for these kinds of joy. Such pleasure cannot exist in a fully optimized world.

4.

Human farmers are inefficient in an optimized world. Human farmers are subject to "bounded rationality." The term was coined by the economist Herbert Simon (who also coined the word "satisficing"), and it describes how individuals are subject to information and time constraints in decision-making. These constraints have enormous impact when you're talking about unanticipated weather events that are only set to increase under climate change. So why not replace the farmers with AI models, which have access to endless data and computation time?

Alibaba is proposing just that, with its ET Agricultural Brain—a hulking new product that uses AI to transform agriculture in order to help create China's pork miracle.

On a gray, chilly day in Hangzhou, I visit Alibaba Cloud to try to understand the company's pledge of using artificial intelligence to help raise pigs in partnership with the Sichuan-based Tequ Group, a sprawling food company with a focus on industrial agriculture. Tequ had pork-yield plans of ten million pigs by 2020 (though they were stymied by failure to contain ASF and labor disruptions from COVID-19). Alibaba Cloud's new campus is a half hour outside the city center, in a place called Cloud Town. The lush green setting reminds me of the Amazon Web Services (AWS) campus in Seattle, including the rain that occasionally pours down in sheets.

The main building is generic, just like the main AWS building, with gray carpets, convenient beverage fridges, and uninspired office furniture. In the main lobby is the Cloud Computing Museum, showcasing Alibaba Cloud's technical achievements of the past decade, which parallel AWS's trajectory.

Online shopping has been the biggest catalyst for innovation over the past twenty years. It's because of online shopping that we have targeted ads, recommendation algorithms, hypnotic social media, and, of course, technical infrastructure for rent from Alibaba Cloud (Aliyun) and AWS. Both these companies started off as e-commerce companies. They leverage shopping lulls on their own platforms to rent out computers, or servers that they aren't using, making money off their unneeded computing power.

Despite increased automation, online shopping still requires legions of engineers. Even the speedy fetching of a high-resolution color image of a product is the result of years of technical innovation. Early e-commerce websites were pretty simple, some text and an image or two. Websites today are increasingly more complex, loaded with 3D videos of products, countless images, interactivity, and algorithms that suggest other products for you. And for a small tech company, instead of running your own servers to host your complex website, renting servers from Aliyun or AWS makes more sense. These costs can balloon into the millions for startups, allowing Alibaba Cloud and AWS to make enormous profits from renting out excess server space. Increasingly, Aliyun and AWS also rent out other tools they've developed internally—voice-recognition tools, satellite imagery, prebuilt AI models. These timeshare computing setups were just as important as venture capital funding in creating the late-2010s tech boom in the United States and China—it's estimated that 40 to 60 percent of all traceable internet traffic now comes from a rented cloud server.

The first wall display at the Cloud Computing Museum describes the platform's initial technical setup. In the early 2000s, a handful of computers sat in the Hangzhou office running Alibaba.com and Taobao.com. While Alibaba.com connected the rest of the world to China's bulk sellers, Taobao.com is a consumer-oriented online shopping platform that is now twice the size of Amazon.

The early Alibaba systems borrowed other people's technology, says the panel, including Oracle databases. The next panel shows a photo taken in 2009 of the smiling faces of Jack Ma and a few engineers holding a computer. The old Oracle databases were replaced by Alibaba's own framework, the Apsara framework, named after the Buddhist goddess of clouds. A towering server sits behind a glass pane, with a printed poem: CODE / LINE BY LINE / BUILDS THE FOUNDATION / FOR ETERNITY / JUST LIKE SAND / GRAIN BY GRAIN / CALMS THE ROARING SEA. Opposite the server are the first lines of code ever run on the Apsara system, configuring logging, heroically presented under a spotlight: Void InitLoggingSystem(conststd::string&configFiles="").

In a brightly lit area painted white, with a half-dead orchid, I sit with Jintong, a stoic Aliyun expert. A few glass-walled conference rooms are down the hall. Jintong tells me that raising pigs using AI was a natural opportunity. The farming structure was already in place; Aliyun just helped optimize it.

Large pork farms already have closed-circuit televisions and sensors, monitored by humans. For a few hundred pigs, a human might do reasonably well overseeing operations. But for hundreds of thousands of pigs, where do you even begin? And in order for China to achieve its pork miracle, millions of pigs *must* be farmed.

Aliyun offers a way to help sort through data using AI. In these large-scale farms, pigs are stamped with a unique identity mark on their bodies, similar to a QR code. That data is fed into a model made by Alibaba, and the model has the information it needs to monitor the pigs in real time, using video, temperature, and sound sensors. It's through these channels that the model detects any sudden signs of fever or disease, or if pigs are crushing one another in their pens. If something does happen, the system recognizes the unique identifier on the pig's body and gives an alert.

Certain machine-learning models, like the one used by ET Agricultural Brain, require massive amounts of training data in order to work. It's only after collecting three months' worth of training data (where cameras sit and record data, without analysis) that the AI model is actually useful. Only then can it be effective in diagnosis.

Jintong explains that, beyond detecting porcine disease, ET Agricultural Brain makes decisions based on data, and offers a precision that is beyond human capacity. ET Agricultural Brain is like a Swiss Army knife of models—these models are fed training data from specific clients, big industrial farms that raise pigs and grow melons, or even agricultural drone companies like XAG, which it helps crunch through sensor data to finesse autopilot capabilities. It can determine the best time to plant, based on the weather, or when to pick fruit for optimal sweetness. ET Agricultural Brain also conveniently plugs into Aliyun's other offerings, like ET Logistics Brain, which can perform complex calculations on the cold chain during food delivery. The problem Matilda posed would be gone with ET Logistics Brain, which would calculate the amount of refrigeration a truck driver had used by sensing how much gas was left in the tank by the end of a trip.

And where are all the human farmers in this scheme? Are they relaxing, eating peanuts as the machines do all the work?

It turns out that humans are still needed. Aliyun works with farmers to formalize their knowledge for the machine-learning models through the Alibaba Knowledge Graph. ET Agricultural Brain can "see," but that is a generous term, given how much effort had to be put into teaching it, and how it can see only a limited set of objects.

But the payoff is enormous—the production of millions of pigs at a low price. Jintong is optimistic that trickle-down innovation can happen. He believes that "dragon-head" agricultural companies, large national conglomerates that rely on a network of smaller farmers, will share certain innovations with their small farmers.

Given the computation time, the data required, the hardware infrastructure needed, and the cost, it currently makes sense to utilize AI only if you are raising millions of pigs, not just one or two. Other companies are also trying to cash in on the AI pork-farming business, using technologies like pig facial recognition.

The logic is striking. A demand for pork drives industrialized farming of pigs, which increases disease transmission. The constant emergence of diseases drives the implementation of new technologies like AI pork farming. These technologies go on to make pork cheap, driving even more availability and demand, as people start to believe pork is a necessary part of their diet. AI is not the balm to any problem—it is just one piece of the ever-hungry quest for scale.

5.

If pig life can be optimized through gene editing and automation, can human life be optimized as well? The concept that human life can be optimized, of human actions being calibrated toward better performance, is a central belief of the ET Agricultural Brain project: it may eventually replace human farmers with AI farmers.

The optimization of life is a distinctly modern endeavor. Some proponents of a world run by artificial intelligence (AI, when a computer program can perform defined tasks as well as humans can) and artificial general intelligence (AGI, computers more powerful than AI, with the ability to understand the world as well as humans can) present an optimized version of human life that is very seductive: rational, error-proof, and objective. Others have similar convictions: if we can quantify human consciousness and emotions through mechanisms like AI, we might be able to reduce suffering by *optimizing* our world to decrease those emotions. One machine-learning engineer I met at a tech salon in San Francisco eagerly described the dawn of this AI world, one without the "clumsy irrationality of meat machines." AI would teach humans how to live ethically and in accordance with reason. "Just imagine," he said, lowering his voice to a hushed tone. He sat uncomfortably close to me, holding a Fibonacci sequence–inspired cocktail, eyes cast intently at my face. "No more irrational things like sexism," he whispered.

Artificial intelligence is a broad category, and that broadness makes it susceptible to slippery usages, to being malleable to any kind of political or economic end. AI is technically a subset of machine learning. And within artificial intelligence, one of the most exciting areas over the past ten years has been work done on neural networks, which are used in deep learning. These artificial neural networks rely on models of the brain that have been formalized into mathematical operations. Research into these "artificial neurons" began as early as 1943, with a paper by Warren McCulloch and Walter Pitts on the perceptron, an algorithm that modeled binary (yes/no) classification, which would serve as the foundation of contemporary neural networks.

Yet the neural networks of today's AI haven't caught up to the latest neuroscience research on how our brains function and process information. And the way brains learn and encode information are still emerging areas of research. One theoretical neuroscientist I spoke to, Ashok Litwin-Kumar, explained that studies and experiments on animal brains are still being done in order to understand more complex, generative brain functions—like constructing new meanings and relationships, or interpreting new experiences. Neurons can be artificially "created" and modeled on a computer, but we still do not know how to regenerate human neurons once they die off. While artificial neural networks often assume there are only a few types of neurons, human neural networks consist of thousands of different types scattered across the body, existing even in places like the stomach. Just replicating a single brain using computer neural networks doesn't guarantee an exact mimicking of brain function. After all, the process of learning doesn't reside solely within our brains; it's environmental, physical, and, most of all, social, carried out through interaction and dialogue.

The seduction of AI is already palpable in China and the United States, across the political spectrum, as people advocate for a fully automated world. The attraction is not simply about rationality and the level of control provided by making systems automated. It's also about scale: once implemented, certain applications of deep learning, like image recognition, have been shown to be faster and more accurate than humans. It's no surprise that these qualities make AI the ideal worker.

Many of us live in a world where machine learning and forms of artificial intelligence already pervade our everyday lives—recommendation algorithms, fun cosmetic and face filters on Snapchat and Meitu, automated checkouts using image-recognition cameras. Since "artificial intelligence" is a vague term, it has become a catchall to instill deep fear of a blurry future. Some radical proponents of AI claim we are on "the edge of a revolution driven by artificial intelligence."[4] These same proponents of the AI revolution espouse the belief that this optimized version of human life will take over, replacing humans in the workplace, as caregivers, or even in romantic relationships. "Artificial" will no longer sit in the term as a dirty caveat. AI will farm greenhouses with data-based decision-making, will drive better, with fewer accidents; AI will make sandwiches and pack boxes. AI will do all this without complaining or needing to sleep.

The philosopher and theorist Sylvia Wynter writes, "The struggle of our new millennium will be one between the ongoing imperative of securing the well-being of our present ethnoclass (i.e., Western bourgeois) conception of the human, Man."[5] Her work deconstructs the way "human" was created as a category. This concept of the "human" was tweaked throughout history to serve the projects of colonialism, slavery, racism, and subjugation. Through religious and economic institutions, the idea of *who* is considered human and *what it means* to be human has for hundreds of years been a political project by those in power. Wynter gives the example of colonial subjects and slaves being designated as nonhuman, with submission leading to salvation, allowing "inferior subjects" to *become human*.

I see the myth of automation replacing humans as yet another attempt by those in power to sharply define the boundaries of what being human means, elevating AI to a form of power that seems to have a righteous, natural force in our lives. This myth defines being human as simply being a rational, efficient worker. The fear instilled by these radical proponents of AI is ominous and forceful, and it implies an inevitability written by those in charge—leaders in the tech world, owners of companies that are building this scary AI. The same fear of automation drives a public discourse that glints with a subterfuge: that being human is the only thing that makes us special.

The project of making AI a natural, evolutionary force continues. In this state of optimized life, we are told humans will be free from work. Silicon Valley claims it has anticipated this mass unemployment by automation, with places like Y Combinator piloting universal basic income programs. Individuals would get a monthly stipend to pay rent and purchase things, keeping a consumer-driven economy afloat. The promise being advertised to us about an AI labor force is that we will be free, and we will also be able to optimize our own tiny human lives—maybe for freedom, for true happiness.

6.

On a subway ride about an hour away from the center of Shanghai, I've struck up a conversation with a kind stranger. I've left Hangzhou, and am headed back to Shanghai for a few days, stopping in villages along the way. Most of my time is spent like this—countryside trips buffered by stops in cities, where I gorge on meals that cost as much as a few months' income for a farmer.

My new acquaintance, Shan, and I sit under neon lights, entranced, watching a video on the subway TV showing how to cook red braised pork. Screens are unavoidable in contemporary Chinese life—they proliferate everywhere, as rampant as the video cameras that are always recording, always watching. For every video camera in a public place, for every surveillance lens watching you, there's a mirror, a screen placed for you to watch ads, cartoons, and news in a hypnotic glaze of content. More than a government conspiracy of surveillance, it ends up feeling like a hardware conspiracy to sell as many video cameras and screens as possible.

Shan is only a few years older than me and has a fifteen-year-old daughter. Shan lives in the center of Shanghai but commutes to the outskirts every day for her job as a database administrator at a motor factory. She's not Christian but she's taking the rest of the day off to make Christmas Eve dinner, for the holiday spirit. She might even make red braised pork.

"Honestly though, over the past few years, Christmas has come and gone. For a while we all celebrated it, even though none of us would call ourselves Christian. But it's different this past year. The government has been seeing it as a Western influence, a religious influence, so you know, they are trying to tamp it down." As rationality and control pervade everyday life in urban China, as life becomes optimized, religion is making a resurgence. Faith can take on new significance in the suspended, static realm of everyday urban life.

In an early work, *Understanding Computers and Cognition*, the computer scientists and AI pioneers Terry Winograd and Fernando Flores point out our tendency to ascribe *rationality* to computers. We do this when a physical system is "so complex, and yet so organized, that we find it convenient, explanatory, pragmatically necessary for prediction, to treat it as if it has beliefs and desires and was rational."

But neither computers nor humans are rational actors—and this *is not* a problem. They continue, "We treat other people not as merely 'rational beings' but as 'responsible beings.' An essential part of being human is the ability to enter into commitments and to be responsible for the courses of action that they anticipate. A computer can never enter into a commitment."[6]

The version of life under AI being sold by big tech companies presents a reassuring, controlled world, where unfettered optimization and automation are inevitable. Those in control, those who built the closed systems of control, unsurprisingly purport to predict the future. As ASF and the number of emerging pathogens climb, it becomes obvious that it is impossible to predict the future because we live in an open system. The imperative for these companies then becomes creating a tighter control loop over all the variables that might exist, making an ever more claustrophobic system. This is the self-fulfilling prophecy of life in an AI world: a static, closed world.

The desire for a controlled world arises from an inability to honor the unknown. "Sometimes we drug ourselves with dreams of new ideas"; we think that "the brain alone will set us free," wrote the poet Audre Lorde in 1977.[7] As a writer and activist, Lorde experienced firsthand the connection between the personal and the political, asking us to question the historically conditioned ways we have been taught to understand the world. "The white fathers told us: 'I think, therefore I am,'" she says, referring to the Enlightenment-era philosophers who dissected knowledge as a technical, mechanical pursuit, rather than seeing forms of knowing as a reservoir of opacity, felt and lived through poetry. She asks us to move beyond dichotomies of rational versus emotional ways of knowing, for "rationality is not unnecessary . . . I don't see feel/think as a dichotomy."[8] Beyond binaries, it is the place of poetry, "that back place, where we keep those unnamed, untamed longings for something different and beyond what is now called possible, to which our analysis and understanding can only build roads." Poetry is a place of power within each of us, and poetry is "the language to express and charter this revolutionary demand, the implementation of that freedom."[9]

I imagine that these tech leaders who envision an AI world also want to get free, they want some kind of freedom, at least for themselves. They claim we will witness freedom from work via robots, allowing us to rethink what it means to be human. And while I see the seductiveness of that proposal, I stray and meander, not to the project of being human, but toward the poetry of living. The end of humanity under AI bears no threat to anything that lies under the baggage of being human: naked, bare life, a responsibility to our lives and others.

On the ground, the bulk of AI research is being carried out by large companies like Alibaba. The realm of AI ethics and public discourse is saturated and funded by those same companies, like Microsoft, Google, and Baidu, and corporations directly manipulate the creation of ethical frameworks.[10] It takes millions of dollars to create AI models like ET Agricultural Brain, and an enormous amount of computation time and data labeling. The economics of these technical requirements concentrate control over these models in a handful of companies. The broader AI industry requires a massive amount of data, and subsequently, companies advocate for lax government restrictions on collecting data. Until the makers and builders of AI solve the material realities of the technology, AI will be stuck in a downward spiral, as a tool to optimize life, shaping it into a closed system. Without questioning the intrinsic faith held in prediction, or the political economies of building algorithms, the field of AI ethics and algorithmic fairness will remain mere fodder for dinner party conversations among the rich.

There is so much potential for AI to serve life, to expand the open systems we do live in. I think of the difference between AI *helping* doctors diagnose and identify disease versus AI *replacing* the human social service worker who determines whether someone should receive medical benefits. Once a model is trained, it can be rapidly deployed and scaled to many communities. There could be scenarios where an AI model helps countless small-scale fisheries across the globe examine weather patterns, getting rid of the need for expensive forms of expertise. This stands in contrast to the current economics of AI, which would lean toward an expensive, corporate AI model that demands small fisheries become industrial fish farms to recuperate costs.

For ET Agricultural Brain, so much labor goes into making the models: not just the labor of engineers at Alibaba, but also the labor of those who create the training data. Farmers examining training data and labeling the pig in the images as sick or healthy. Entire swaths of Guiyang designated as "digital towns," where young rural migrants sit and generate training data for AI, clicking on images, tagging animals and objects. Despite stories of AI replacing humans, AI still desperately needs us.

That is the reality of work and labor. For more than twenty-five years, my mother woke up at 4:00 a.m. and drove to her job as a university cafeteria worker outside Boston. She used to have a deep commitment to her job, and it gave her a sense of fulfillment. It felt good to feed stressed-out college students who weren't taking care of themselves. She and her coworkers were trusted by management, given breaks and autonomy on the job.

Over the past ten years, her feelings of fulfillment have drastically turned. The school *optimized* her work with arbitrary, quantitative metrics. As a result of this optimization process, there's less autonomy, fewer breaks, and new, bizarre working schedules. My mother feels little connection to her job now. My mother's is the kind of job that some people think robots should take over, that should be optimized and automated. After all, she would supposedly get more free time and fulfillment in life. The irony is, she stopped feeling fulfilled when her workplace became optimized, her work stripped of meaning, turned into mere labor.

Examining the relationship between work and life under automation is not new. In a 1972 article in *The Black Scholar*, the activist James Boggs argued for the importance of thinking one level deeper about *work* itself. The problem facing jobs and work isn't merely "automation and cybernation," as he put it. Instead, the real challenge is "to create a new human meaning for *Work as Working for others rather than for oneself*; *working for people* rather than *for things*." Transforming work into abstract, quantifiable, optimized labor erases "any of the human and social purposes or the creative satisfactions that Work has always had in other societies."[11] It is easy to automate work using AI once you've made work devoid of meaning.

Like so many AI projects, ET Agricultural Brain naively assumes that the work of a farmer is to simply produce food for people in cities, and to make the food cheap and available. In this closed system, feeding humans is no different from feeding swaths of pigs on large farms. The project neglects the real work of smallholder farmers throughout the world. For thousands of years, the work of these farmers has been stewarding and maintaining the earth, rather than optimizing agricultural production. They use practices that yield nutrient-dense food, laying a foundation for healthy soils and rich ecology in an uncertain future. Their work is born out of commitment and responsibility: to their communities, to local ecology, to the land. Unlike machines, these farmers accept the responsibility of their actions with the land. They commit to the path of uncertainty.

After all, life is defined not by uncertainty itself but by a commitment to living despite it. In a time of economic and technological anxiety, the questions we ask cannot center on the inevitability of a closed system built by AI, and how to simply make those closed systems more rational or "fair." What we face are the more difficult questions about the meaning of work, and the ways we commit, communicate, and exist in relation to each other. Answering these questions means looking beyond the rhetoric sold to us by tech companies. What we stand to gain is nothing short of true pleasure, a recognition that we are not isolated individuals, floating in a closed world.

As the subway gets closer to Shanghai, it weaves past rivers and farmland. More and more passengers get on, more and more apartment buildings appear out the window. It gets louder, with teenagers in their school uniforms getting on the train, watching videos on their phones. An old grandmother holds her grandson's Totoro backpack as he nibbles a wafer. Shan's stop is coming up. She gives me a big, encouraging smile before she walks out of the subway car. "Merry Christmas!" she says. "Don't spend it alone!"

.4.

Buffet Life

1.

Sun Wei is twenty-five years old. He's portly, with a pleasant, round face and a slight lisp, sporting a short ponytail with a shaved undercut. He's on the phone, nodding vigorously in a deferential tone to the person on the other end. When he's done, he starts to tell me about his path to becoming one of the few licensed drone operators in the country and the founder of his own farm service company.

I met him at Hotel Nikko in Guangzhou, for the XAG Drone Users Conference. XAG is an agricultural drone company, making drones that map fields and perform precision pesticide spraying of crops. The company's new headquarters is in a part of the city that is wildly empty, a new "high-tech industry area," which so many cities across China are now building. The push in Guangzhou toward high-tech industries is an attempt to strengthen the Greater Bay Area of Shenzhen, Guangzhou, and Hong Kong into an economic powerhouse.

It's advantageous for XAG to be out here. There are few buildings around—it's mainly mountains and construction sites. XAG has ambitious plans for new precision agriculture plots and vegetable beds outside its headquarters, for testing out new features on its drones. Its biggest competitor is DJI, a "unicorn" company valued at US$15 billion, just two hours away in nearby Shenzhen.

The first thing I notice while talking to Wei is his optimism about the future. He's from a small town in Anhui Province, and he exudes a contagious happiness about his present situation—a gratitude for all the luck that's befallen him. I feel happy basking in this energy.

When American headlines talk of trade war and American decline due to China, maybe it's this kind of energy that pundits are referring to. It's a feeling that you have a right to the future, a right to imagination beyond the immediacy of the day—a feeling that may never have been in the United States to begin with but that, we are told by the media, is disappearing. I think back to one summer, driving across California through rural counties. Stopping at a Walmart, I watched a young woman with a blond ponytail explaining the features of a floor mop she was holding. "It can even go in the wash!" she chirped theatrically, peeling back the Velcro attachment. "Saves you time, and we all know there's not enough time these days. I'm a public school teacher during the week, but I'm workin' it, even though it's a weekend." Her cheerful tone reflected a mixture of pride and acceptance in having to work constantly just to scrape by.

Looking at Wei's face and his relaxed smile, I see someone who strongly believes he has the right to a future, a future that is not steeped in precariousness, or in working weekends at a Walmart in rural Anhui. He's enormously modest, but his life might be a parable about an emerging Chinese Dream wrought by rural education and community support. It also speaks to the stark line that emerges: between those who fund code, and those who write and use code.

Wei had a vocational high school education, never making it to college. Few of the kids he grew up with ever did. His dad worked for the state-owned railroad as a mechanic, and at some point, he was expected to take over his father's post. This is fairly typical when someone in the family has a solid, working-class government job with good benefits—an "iron rice bowl." There're still a lot of jobs like this in China, considered to be good positions in the remnants of socialism. Stable hours, guaranteed retirement at age sixty, great health care, and a solid pension.

These jobs go hand in hand with the infrastructure and architecture that was built during high socialism, a passing reminder of the once grand ambitions of socialism to imagine a completely new society. Central heating is a good example, where each concrete residential building block in northern China had its heat turned on at the same time, controlled by a city furnace. An uncle of mine was a central heating technician for a long time, a job he inherited from my grandfather. My cousin, growing up under the promises of the free market, wanted something more glamorous. Instead of becoming a central heating technician, he opened his own car dealership, using money he borrowed from family members. He's now a proud *tuhao* (nouveau riche, 土豪) who owns multiple Louis Vuitton bags purchased from his travels to Paris.

Wei was equally disinterested in his dad's position, and his parents contemplated sending him into the military. But Wei had access to the internet. He discovered the world of model planes and helicopters, building his own from instructional videos online, and connecting with enthusiasts over chat. This eventually led him to discover XAG drones, and the XAG drone-pilot training program, run through WeChat.

There are about thirty thousand drone operators in China, and increasing demand for them. Before starting his own farm service company, Wei worked with a different group of farm service technicians in Anhui. Since the 1990s, small farm service teams have formed across rural China, as a response to the needs of a changing countryside. While farms stayed small, the loss of agricultural labor to urban areas meant a demand for help and labor on farms. Agricultural service teams started forming, both buying and making their own equipment that would work on these small-scale farms, helping farm owners harvest as well as spray pesticides and fertilizers throughout the year. These service teams are not just hired help, though—they are often at the front lines of developing new tools and new farm machinery, a goal that is part of the ambitious Made in China 2025 Plan to catalyze China into a knowledge- and service-based economy.

Wei says what distinguishes his farm service team from others is not just the use of drones, but the way drones attract a crew of motivated young people. The majority of these young people are from rural areas. They are excited about learning new digital skills rather than farming the way their parents did. During peak season, the farm service team members work long, tireless days. After the harvest, Wei takes some time off and works with XAG directly to train new drone operators and talk to potential drone buyers.

This year, Wei has driven more than thirty thousand kilometers in his SUV, working all across the country. Since the demand for drone operators is high, he helped spray crops everywhere from his home province of Anhui to the cotton fields of Xinjiang. He says he loves all the travel, and the unexpected situations that arise on the job—drone breakdowns with immediate fixes required in remote regions.

I imagine Wei's story in California, the largest agriculture-producing state in the United States, with its markedly different system of industrial-farming infrastructure. And as someone wary of stories where tech seems to magically transform lives, I have my doubts about if, and how, this model of entrepreneurship might scale. Yet I can't help but admit that his path is inspiring. To meet someone who grew up with the expectation that he would have to take over a stale job, but who now runs his own agricultural service team using drones, making more money than his parents, is the kind of dream story that would be advertised all over San Francisco as a billboard for the gig economy. I can imagine the ad on BART trains: *No college education? No problem. Turn your passion for flying remote controlled airplanes into a career as a drone pilot. Be your own boss. Support local farmers. It's a win-win.*

I don't know if Wei is truly his own boss, but I do know that he is now someone else's boss, someone's teacher and mentor. Unlike in the gig economy, his wages are not determined by an algorithm, nor did he swap a human boss for a computer one. He had, in the parlance of contemporary white-collar jobs, "opportunities for growth." Rather than seeing him and others like him as mere drone operators or contractors, XAG takes the feedback of its drone pilots seriously, involving them in the process of updating drone hardware and features. He also wouldn't be where he is now without the luxury that most Chinese parents traditionally offer their children: free room and board until they get married.

Most of all, it's clear to me that Wei just loves drones, and he genuinely loves being part of XAG. While the gig economy workers I've talked to see themselves as free agents, temporarily making money under a company they typically were ambivalent about, Wei was excited by XAG. One of his hobbies is photography, and he's developed a reputation with XAG marketing as a top-notch drone photographer. He shows me images of beautiful rice paddies and swaths of wheat. He often sends the marketing department his favorite photos just for fun.

Wei's not alone at this conference. About half the attendees are drone operators from farm service companies, from all areas of China. The drone operators are distinct in a sea of people, darkened from the sun, greeting each other in a twangy rural dialect that veers off the accepted national standards of Mandarin pronunciation.

One farm service company owner tells me that while many farmers were at first suspicious of drones, they eventually realized how cost-effective drones are. Since the drones are more precise in their application of pesticides and fertilizers, farmers could save money on material costs. "Farmers think it's really fashionable to use drones now, and they will tell their neighbors all about it," the farm service company owner says. As of 2018, 5 percent of farming in China was done using precision agriculture. XAG drones are typically used by farms around three hectares in size, because of hardware constraints. Since 98 percent of farm households own small pieces of land less than two hectares, there remains ample room for market growth. With this potential boom and the scalability of Wei's drone-pilot training, I wonder how long the field will continue to grow before there is an oversaturation of drone operators.

2.

The drone user conference is a cross section of Chinese technology and the dynamics of contemporary life in China. Investors and venture capitalists sit at the very front, their neatly pressed clothing and stylish haircuts alluding to wealthy ease. Thin, fit thought leaders in T-shirts are behind them, along with some of the guest speakers at the conference—business development execs from Ant Financial and Alibaba, Bayer Crop Science and academics. They have undergone schooling at top universities such as Tsinghua and Peking University, or have degrees from places abroad like Australia, England, and the United States. Behind the thought leaders and guests are one or two engineers who work at XAG and, of course, the press. Two young women from CCTV Channel 7, the national military and agricultural channel, sit looking despondently bored, trying to stay awake. One of them starts to nod off in the afternoon.

A wide aisle separates the farm service company owners and drone operators, who sit in the back. That's where Sun Wei is, along with Lei Bing, who I also met earlier—he's a taciturn drone operator who is my age but looks ten years older, renowned in the community for his fierce piloting on steep terrain. It's rowdy in the back of the auditorium. During the new-feature unveiling for the latest drone model by XAG's CTO, there's a nonstop buzz of voices. When the automatically refillable tank for pesticides is announced, the front of the auditorium politely claps while the crowd in the back stands up, fists pumping, "Finally! Finally you heard us!" The CTO points to increased sensors on the drone, and the drone operators cheer and clap loudly like sports spectators. New modular components that click together are announced, meaning no more fumbling with tiny screws in the middle of a field, and the operators lose it, hooting and hollering so loudly that it puts smirks on the faces of the well-heeled crowd up front.

The one time the farm service teams and drone operators stay silent is when the CTO announces that they are working on a simplified drone navigation system, so that the farmers themselves can fly the drones instead of relying on technical teams. Operators have a look of concern about the future of their own jobs. The CTO seems to have anticipated this and assures everyone that this is actually good news for the drone operators. When farmers become drone operators, drone operators can then move on to more high-level tasks, like data management, mapping, and business strategy. Along the rungs of drone life, everyone can expect to move up and advance, year by year.

I ask Sun Wei his opinion about the equalizing effects of technology, if a technical position like his is liberating and will allow him to do anything he wants in the future. These equalizing effects are pervasive throughout the technology and development world, the stories of "technology transforming lives" tiresome in their ubiquity. Projects like the failed One Laptop per Child, by Nicholas Negroponte, or the Hole in the Wall project exude this techno-optimistic belief—if you can give a laptop to a child or put a computer in an Indian slum, children will teach themselves linear algebra and become the next Bill Gates. We now know this is a myth inflated by a hype cycle. A whole support system of teachers, peers, and family is a stronger influence than a laptop or computer screen. But part of me—the American part of me—wants to believe the narrative about individualistic passion overcoming everything, including a lack of formal schooling or connections.

Sun Wei grins at my question and gives me a pitying look. He says, "Of course not. I have old teammates that went to Beida and unlike us *diaosi* [literally "pubic hair," slang for loser], they're off getting big promotions and roles with more responsibility. They have good backgrounds, they studied engineering. I just studied drone flying."

Wei's story might become increasingly common,

though. One focus of recent government policy is to decrease the gap between rural and urban schools by using a wide variety of methods, including livestreaming classes, increased off-line vocational education, and massive online open courses. Some of these online education initiatives are private, sponsored by companies including Alibaba and NetEase, and others are experiments in public education. XAG itself is partnering with Zhonghang Future (中航未来教育集团) to roll out a massive virtual online flight school as well as a hundred thousand physical flight schools across the country. By the end of 2018, more than twenty thousand people had finished the online training portion through WeChat. And if XAG does intend for existing farmers to become drone operators, and for existing drone operators to become geographic information data managers, will these internet-enabled, distance-learning initiatives work? Will they be more successful than previous models of development through technology?

3.

The city of Chengdu in Sichuan Province might be known to Americans for its spicy food and pandas, but in China, Chengdu is known for its Number 7 High School. Chengdu Number 7 High School is famous for its academic performance. It's a public school that boasts a 99 percent college-entrance rate, including graduates who go on to places such as UC Berkeley, Harvard, and MIT. Some of its students are winners of international math and science contests, and have gone on to participate in the Olympics, and the school has a wide array of extracurricular activities, including a high school orchestra that has toured globally.

In the viral online article "This Screen Changes Lives," the writer Cheng Mengchao documents a grand experiment carried out by Chengdu Number 7 High School—a decision in 2015 to livestream the school's classes to seventy-two thousand students in poverty-stricken rural areas of Yunnan and Guangxi with the help of New Oriental Education, an edtech (educational technology) company based in Beijing.[1] The initial results were dire: rural teachers tore books up in protest, resentful of being replaced by Chengdu teachers on a digital screen. Rural students would unexpectedly burst into tears of frustration, confronted with how behind they were compared to city students at the same grade level. "I didn't know I was so bad in school, I didn't know I was so worthless," remarked one student.

While more than 40 percent of Americans receive some kind of education after high school, only 10 percent of rural Chinese do. Even finishing high school is rare in rural China, where the dropout rate in middle school is 50 percent, and the high school dropout rate is as high as 66 percent. These rural students face the pressure of taking a job to support their families rather than spending their time in school. Part of this also has to do with self-image: parents and students themselves often hold the belief that they're just not "suited to studying."

Three years after the first classes were broadcast on livestream in Chengdu, there is a glimmer of hope. The first college-entrance exam results are promising. In previous years, only two students from these rural areas went to top universities in China. After the three-year experiment, eighty-eight students were headed to Tsinghua and Peking University. One rural student received his Peking University acceptance notice while working alongside his father on a construction site.

Li Miao, a professor at Shandong University who studies rural education via livestream, emphasizes that the material conditions surrounding these rural students are still difficult to overcome. For example, many students are often late to school or miss portions of a lesson just because the school outhouse is located far away. And while cell phones, tablets, and 5G internet are common throughout rural China, these devices do not change a prevailing attitude within families that education is a privilege rather than a necessity.

4.

Why would the Chinese government put so much effort into bridging the gap between rural and urban education? Rather than its being an act of sheer benevolence, or solely an iron fist on the valve of economic growth, the reality is that those in power want to stay in power.

For a long time, rural migrants ages eighteen to forty-five headed to the city, working and receiving higher incomes than they would in their hometowns, but not enough money to tether themselves to the city—to put down roots or buy property. In several studies, young migrants said they felt deeply unwelcome in the cities they were working in. They also felt a deep sense of alienation, lacking access to the traditional markers of adulthood such as being able to afford a house or car. The choices they had, between life in the city and life back home, were limited. In 2017, the particular plight of migrants became amplified when a fire tore through a migrant-worker village in Beijing. Such migrant-worker villages are known throughout China as "urban villages." The Beijing city government termed these migrant workers a "low-end population" that would have to be removed. The city deemed these urban villages an eyesore as an excuse to demolish the villages and displace the migrants.

This large mass of people moving back and forth from city to countryside is a potential powder keg. Young, able-bodied workers, especially young men, untethered from car or house ownership, job, or family are threats to political stability. So the government is betting on Rural Revitalization in hopes of attracting young people back to their homes, where they will be under the watchful eye of elders, or at least have some kind of attachment, some commitment to place. This "re-peasantization" process is having mixed results. Rural opportunity can't rely solely on fiscal incentives, so a whole infrastructure of education and new types of livelihoods are being created for those who decide to return.

So far, China's strategy of becoming the world's largest economy has been about quantity—relying on the economics of scale and its vast population. But the reality of manufacturing is that there is always somewhere cheaper to make things. In order for China to truly reach sustainable economic success, to move more people into the middle class, it needs a populace with a higher level of education.

The head of international marketing at XAG, Anne, is thirty years old. She's an ikebana enthusiast and could easily fit in at a tech company in San Francisco. Originally born and raised in Guangzhou, she is also a returnee. After spending a few years abroad, studying in the U.K., she returned home to Guangzhou for the increased opportunities here.

The conference lunch at Hotel Nikko is a buffet, a lavish display of excess. It includes an abundance of meat and seafood, prepared in a myriad of ways, from braised beef and fried chicken to coarse chunks of sushi, crudely cut. The buffet lunch requires a strategy for how much you can possibly eat while getting your money's worth. Meat and seafood rank at the top of getting the best value, fruit and vegetables at the bottom. The thought leaders and venture capitalists (VCs) at the conference are unfazed by the display of plenty, having access to luxuries at any time. I see a few of them at a corner table, sipping tea, picking at the edges of a bowl of rice, frenetically talking about business yields and the next quarter.

Anne and I are wedged into a corner of the lobby. Next to our table is a quiet Japanese journalist who casually mentions that he is going to Xinjiang next week to report on precision agriculture in the region, a tumultuous part of the country that is responsible for 84 percent of China's cotton production—no small feat given China's status as the world's second-largest cotton producer. When I ask if he speaks Mandarin or Uyghur, he shakes his head, holds up his phone, and says, "Google translate."

At our table, Anne and I talk about returning home, and where that sense of home comes from. It's clear from the way she talks about home that the feeling of belonging somewhere is important to her. This value comes out especially when she talks about young drone pilots returning home. "Plant protection with drones is a new profession that gives rural people enough income to survive while staying in their hometown to be with their families. They are working with dignity and respect. That's why it's driving more and more people to return to their hometown. And we are very glad to see this happen."

But is it enough to lure young people back to the countryside?

Buffet life is a whole other realm, far from the countryside with its small plates of food and limited choice. As we sit and eat our lunch, I watch the drone operators joke and laugh, plates piled high with emptied crab shells, shrimp heads, and fish bones. One man slaps his friend on the back, smiling and heartily saying, "See? People live the good life here in Guangzhou! Now we get to experience it!"

How to Eat Yourself

Cloud computing is a nasty business. Despite its airy name, its data centers, with their numerous computer servers, rely on massive amounts of energy and resources, making up 2 percent of the world's electricity use. That percentage is only expected to grow with increased global traffic. A few cloud computing companies are now purchasing carbon offsets to become "greener," although some accuse the move of fueling inequality, allowing rich developed countries to purchase their way out of their responsibility for pollution. Usually located in rural regions, data centers also use a range of rare earth minerals, which have a particularly bad reputation for the environmental impact of their mining. As a result, researchers are looking into alternative, environmentally friendly ways of storing the world's massively growing data. In 2017, Microsoft researchers began pioneering a way to store data inside DNA, a method far more efficient than using computer servers. This recipe envisions a future in which GMO foods and DNA data storage come together. If you truly were your user data, could you eat yourself?

Ingredients for the Soy Milk

dried soybeans | 150 g

water | At least 2,000 ml, depending on how thick you like your soy milk. Add more for a thinner, less "beany" soy milk.

Ingredients for the Fritters

tofu, silken texture | approximately 400 g

mayonnaise | 120 g

cornstarch | 60 g

salt | to taste, about 11 g

oil | for frying, depending on your preference, canola/peanut, etc.

green onions | for garnish, optional, sliced finely

Tools

electric blender

fine cheesecloth

In the late 2030s, companies turned toward DNA as a far cheaper, more sustainable, more space-saving way of storing data than the previous model of cold storage on computers. A few years later, BGI Genomics based out of Shenzhen announced that in partnership with Bayer Crop Science, genetically modified crops such as soybeans and corn could now be encoded with data inside their DNA.

Farms planting GMO soybeans could now have an extra source of income. They could collaborate with large cloud storage companies to plant soybean data fields with customer data encoded inside each bean. Strict data localization laws are common throughout the world, where data must be physically kept within the country's borders for security purposes. As a result, the Chinese Ministry of Technology and Ministry of Agriculture saw an opportunity to combine two systems of security into one: food security with data localization. Soybean reserves could also be data reserves.

Unlike cold computer storage, DNA storage has a long half-life, of five hundred years. An economically feasible method of data destruction had to be devised. Researchers came up with a solution: cloud soybeans with embedded data are sold to the public for a highly discounted price. After these beans are digested, the data becomes thoroughly obliterated, ensuring data privacy.

Soybeans are enormously versatile. While soybeans were manually ground in ancient times throughout East Asia, electric blenders are now used instead for home soy-milk making. After the soy milk is made, different kinds of tofu can also be produced from the milk, and the soybean lees (pulp) leftover from the milk-making process can be turned into delicious fritters.

Although you can choose to consume whatever data you'd like, the flavor of cloud soybeans comes from the data content. Is it a photo of yourself with a bad haircut from five years ago, or a flattering headshot from your LinkedIn profile? Or is it yesterday's newspaper headlines? For this recipe, we suggest going with a neutral-flavored data soybean, maybe some shipping transactions on a ledger or your to-do list from a few years ago. Or, for the brave, archived personal e-mails give the fritters a complex, heavy flavor with extra-crunchy texture.

To Make the Soy Milk

To start off, sort the beans carefully. Make sure to take out any green or non-yellow soybeans—this is a sign of bit rot in the data. Put the beans in a large glass bowl and soak overnight.

The next day, drain the beans. Blend on high for several minutes. You should have a liquid with a pulpy, smoothie-like texture.

Put the contents of the blender into a large pot. Bring the soy milk mixture to a boil, then simmer for 10 minutes. Keep a close eye on the pot, as soy milk bubbles over easily! The mixture is ready when foam appears on top. Make sure that the soybean liquid is properly cooked through—that it has reached a boil and simmered for at least 10 minutes—as uncooked soybeans cause indigestion.

Now separate the liquid (milk) from the crushed soybeans. (Be careful not to burn yourself with the hot liquid!) Separate the two by placing cheesecloth over a container and pouring the contents of the pot onto the cheesecloth. One method is to place the cheesecloth over a colander, which sits on top of a container. Squeeze and strain out the solids, using a utensil to help mash and strain (so that you don't have to use your hands). Set aside the solids.

Pour the milk back into the large pot for the second cooking. Make sure to stir frequently so that it doesn't burn. Bring the milk to a boil and then lower to a simmer. A light skin will start to form at the top. Skim the skin off and save it—it's a delicious, tender bean curd, and considered a delicacy!

The milk is now ready to be diluted or sweetened, according to taste.

To Make the Fritters

Mash together the leftover soybean lees with the tofu, mayonnaise, and cornstarch. Salt to taste. Shape into small balls.

In a wok, heat up enough oil that it will cover the fritters. Place the fritters into the wok and fry at medium heat until the outsides become crispy golden brown. Remove from the heat using a slotted spoon and place onto napkins. These fritters are great with any kind of dipping sauce.

Note that fritters are just one of many possible recipes for the soybean lees! The lees is great in savory egg pancakes, mixed with rice and fried into cakes, or stewed with dates, rice, and whatever your heart desires.

.5.

Made in China

1.

On the windowsill of the house I'm staying at, there is a tiny toy bird. It fits in the palm of my hand, and is made out of plastic and Styrofoam, with some natural materials tacked on to it—a tail made out of wood, seeds for eyes, pieces of a pine cone turned into a regal plume. On the bottom of the bird, a small round sticker says *Made in China*.

Even out here, in a small Northern California town with a thousand people, the words are inescapable. I feel flushed with embarrassment as I place the bird back on the windowsill, but I keep knocking it over during the rest of my visit.

During the stirrings of the Chinese economic boom in the 1990s, my uncle helped run an import-export business that sold millions of small birds like these. My uncle would frequently fly from the Pearl River Delta to the United States for trade shows, bringing sample boxes of fake birds, fake flowers, small baskets, little Styrofoam mushrooms and gnomes. He'd stay with my family for a few days, enjoying my mother's cooking instead of the American fast food available on the road. Sometimes he would leave extra boxes of these trade show samples with us, no longer useful once deals were made. Stuck to them were always the words *Made in China*. These three words held a strong gravity, cast a magical spell. I would marvel at these items, sensing the strange, enchanting edges of materialism.

A few of these small birds ended up at a street stall in Boston that another aunt of mine ran on the weekends. On a low table with a white tablecloth she laid out her wares: jade pendants, wooden fans, all kinds of chinoiserie you'd find at stores with names like Eastern Trading Co. I brought her these trade show leftovers, on a weekend when I was helping her. I had schemes to help my aunt sell more of her goods. As a recent immigrant, she knew very little English, so I wrote several signs to put in front of the items, in flowery language: BEAUTIFUL, EXOTIC, HANDMADE, JADE PENDANT . . .

Later in the day, an older couple briefly stopped. I beamed. They smiled back and after examining our table, they left, the husband pushing his wife along. "Don't fall for that stuff, it's cheap, made in China," I heard him say. For a moment, I didn't know if he meant the objects on the table or me.

As a ten-year-old kid, I found his reaction perplexing and nonsensical. In the 1990s, what was seen as Chinese culture was still a product of the American imagination. I was made fun of every day for the "weird food" I'd bring for lunch. Chinese restaurants were still serving General Tso's chicken and chop suey, without the elevation of San Francisco's Mister Jiu's. People who stopped at our stand didn't even know what jade was, and often asked me if it was glass. Even if our stall sold the highest-quality jade and we demanded more money for it, customers would be unable to judge the quality themselves, and would become convinced that we were trying to swindle them. A lot of people already thought we were trying to swindle them, by virtue of being Chinese. So of course we sold the lowest-quality jade, hoping at least someone, maybe entranced by the green-blue swirl of color, would find the low price a little easier to entertain and make a harmless impulse purchase.

Made in China became seared into my psyche as a symbol of corruptness. The phrase meant something shoddily crafted, made by people who were mindless drones in a factory bent on gaining profit by cheating foreigners out of an extra cent or two. I could imagine these people at one of the factories my uncle worked with, eyes glazed over, mindlessly gluing pine-cone pieces onto a Styrofoam bird. It reflected the laziness of the Chinese, who were unwilling to consider the notion of perfection and craft, people who were culturally unable to be diligent about work and always wanted to cut corners. It was made by people who looked like me, people who could be related to me—distant cousins and aunts from my family's ancestral home. My childhood optimism pitted against the man's proclamation transformed *Made in China* into the three most shameful words I could think of.

For millions of people across rural China, from places like Anhui, where Sun Wei the drone operator is from, *Made in China* changed lives. It allowed young women to move to cities and experience freedom from overbearing, patriarchal elders for the first time, as Leslie T. Chang and Ching Kwan Lee document in their work on factory girls—young women who moved to cities by themselves, working in factories, living in factory dorms. It restructured families, labor, and political power. It was innovation in the purest sense of the word: an economic and technological shift that reshaped the social fabric of the country, for better and worse. And now, *Made in China* is being redefined again, this time by the countryside.

2.

The sprawling Tianjin Museum is new, a striking building in the middle of a concrete plaza. It reflects Tianjin's cosmopolitan ambitions as part of the Beijing-Tianjin-Hebei (Jingjinji) economic zone. An exhibit on the third floor documents more than three hundred years of history, from the 1600s to modern-day China. Tianjin was formerly a treaty port, and this exhibition has special significance, showing the geography of Tianjin divided under Western powers.

An old map of the city sits in the large atrium, along with images of Tianjin in rubble. On one wall a prominently displayed list lays out the ways native Tianjiners were treated as second-class citizens in their own country. One glass exhibition case emphasizes something even more humiliating: the weapons used by Chinese armies in fighting against Western forces. On one side of the display is an elegant rifle that belonged to a British general. On the other side are a few machetes, some arrows, and a crude gun with a short barrel that belonged to Chinese troops. For a country that invented gunpowder, the set of arrows is laughable.

In the 1960s, the historian Joseph Needham proposed a question: "Why did China never develop modern science?" Despite forward-thinking achievements such as complex geometry as early as 100 B.C.E., China failed to develop science and technology any further after the sixteenth century C.E. Needham's question continues to haunt discussions in the United States on Chinese innovation.

Try searching "China" and "innovation" online, and instead of finding articles about innovations from China, you'll see articles that examine "Why China can't innovate." The answers ultimately all converge on what Needham saw as a key barrier to Chinese innovation: its culture. Needham saw the ancient Taoism that haunted China as the problem—the sleepy Eastern belief that the universe is already perfect: we simply have to maintain the balance. This type of thinking was antithetical to the project of innovation.

The word "innovation" is laden with baggage. It gives rise to a whole industry built on conferences, media, and thought leadership. It's not clear what exactly innovation is, but whatever it is, there is apparently a paucity of this golden resource everywhere except Silicon Valley.

In English, "innovation" was not always regarded as positively as it is now. Its original form in Latin means "to *renew*, to introduce something *as new*," perhaps subliminally acknowledging that the category "entirely new" is difficult to define. The word "innovation" was derogatory in the age of monarchs, as it referred to political and economic change that could bring down empires, threatening the status of kings and elites. But slowly, throughout the Industrial Revolution, the phrase began to be seen as more positive when engineering culture took shape. In the early 1900s, Thorstien Veblen advocated the idea that technology was the output, the *product* of a group of male workers he termed "engineers."[1] And while engineers worked to create technology, it was the company owners, the grand industrialists, who reaped the profits of innovation.

Contemporary innovation in the United States and China appears to strengthen rather than threaten the political and economic order of the world. Riffling through recent coverage on innovation shows the most innovative products appear to be varying forms of management through technology—managing people, cars, take-out orders, or goods. Our modern-day monarchs, corporations and CEOs, are unthreatened by innovation. It begs the question: If innovation is so disruptive, why would it be embraced by people with so much to lose?

3.

In an attempt to find out what "innovation" really means, I meet up with an analyst from one of the largest trans-Pacific VC firms, with a portfolio of companies and products that you've definitely used. It's a hybrid Chinese-U.S. firm and reflects the changing geographies of a trans-Pacific elite. This analyst is young, fresh-faced, and has an intimidating confidence that makes me feel ten years her junior. We know each other through a shared alma mater, but we otherwise have little in common. Her worldview has a ruthless clarity while I am still waffling on the definition of the word "innovation."

I meet her at a yogurt place in Palo Alto. We sit, and I pick at my sad cup of handmade, oddly chunky yogurt. We end up talking about food. She gleefully tells me about her habit of buying ice cream from Taobao.com. For her, the information asymmetry of not knowing, as a consumer, the quality of the goods you'll receive feels resolved by the purchasing of food on the internet. Justice is dealt to sellers through bad reviews.

One hindrance to Chinese innovation has been the accusation that any technological advancement boils down to a government conspiracy to surveil its citizens. The analyst shakes her head, perplexed by the American obsession with the Chinese surveillance state, while Americans seem to care so little about the surveillance in their own lives. We talk about the Silicon Valley hubris that keeps people from digging too deeply into Chinese technology with an honest look: Silicon Valley is the peak of innovation, so how could another place surpass it? On the other side of hubris is a rhetorical trap: China as a constructed enemy for the American government, in order for it to catalyze domestic support for a range of policies by inciting old-fashioned, U.S.A.-brand nationalism. It's not surprising that tech CEOs like Mark Zuckerberg use China as a straw man, arguing that stringent government regulation will prevent American companies from moving fast. Even in narratives of Chinese economic might, China is not innovative; rather, it steals, it cheats, it oppresses.

After the People's Republic of China was founded, science and technology research did take a slow start. According to Barry Naughton and Chen Ling, the state held tight institutional control over research and development. But in the 2000s, R&D shifted, spilling out into the private realm—highlighted by the success of early internet startups with private investment in China, such as Sohu and Baidu. At the same time, the economic success of Town and Village Enterprises showed how new institutional structures could catalyze innovation. And for many companies in China at the time, innovation wasn't about creating entirely new products—"disruptive innovation"—but also about the ways existing processes could be optimized and streamlined, a form of "continuous innovation."

By the 2000s, foreign companies had entered China. These companies still dominate the majority of certain sectors in China, despite purportedly extensive intellectual property theft. They are typically not tech companies—examples are Procter & Gamble, Coca-Cola, and KFC.

Foreign tech firms, however, failed to take off in China, for the same reason China itself is unable to innovate: culture. Companies like eBay floundered in China, straining under the local advantage that Taobao had in understanding the Chinese market. Key details were missed, including the fact that eBay brokers secondhand goods, but in China, buying secondhand goods, especially clothing, is frowned upon. Even when Google left China, it had only 33 percent of market share. The great innovators of the United States found that innovation was culturally constructed. Technology and innovation were far less universal than they had thought.

"I think China is innovating," the VC analyst tells me. "I have American apps that I open once a month and eventually delete. But there are Chinese apps that I open multiple times a day. You're so dependent on apps for daily life. There's a saying about 'China speed'—that tech in China is moving so fast that America can barely keep up." For this analyst, these apps, their convenience, indicate that disruptive innovation is happening in China.

A friend of mine, a VC who spends ample time traveling between the United States and China, remarks that the Silicon Valley hubris is real. He tells me that most of the time, you hear people say they're starting the new Silicon Valley of somewhere, and it never happens, it fails. As a result, Silicon Valley's mythological standing only gets greater and greater. But what lies at the heart of Silicon Valley's greatness, for him, is actually the embrace of failure. This embrace of failure is very much cultural. And in China, he's observed an increased tolerance for risk, for failure, alongside an increased set of innovations. This increased tolerance for risk is pervasive: from young students willing to forgo a steady job in order to start their own companies, against the traditional grain of Chinese society's expectations, to risky leaps in product development, investment, and lending practices.

For both this young analyst and my VC friend, innovation still seems to carry a lot of assumptions. Why does the new, the novel, always require a certain amount of addiction to an app? If failure is so important for innovation, why are we only confronted with stories of technology's successes, rather than stories of its spectacular technical failures? If embracing failure is the prerequisite for innovation, who has the privilege of failing? In Mao's ill-guided experiment in the Great Leap Forward, failure meant famine and death. For students in contemporary rural China, failure means the difference between a life of difficult manual labor, and a vague shot at being able to escape poverty. As China's P2P (peer-to-peer) lending scandals unfold, they show that investing and failure are markedly different when it's a VC firm taking the risk versus a seventy-year-old retiree. And for investment firms, failure can still be lucrative. Failure in the land of contemporary VC-driven innovation seems like a cocktail hour, albeit a grueling one.

There are also the technical realities of innovation. One AI engineer I met, based in Zhongguancun, the "Silicon Valley of China," scoffs at the idea of indigenous Chinese innovation. In a deadpan tone, she points out that China still relies on American chip manufacturers, while American chip manufacturers rely on Chinese rare earth mines. Even the chip engineers are an international community and chip factories are all across the globe. Indigenous innovation is just a nationalist parlor trick.

4.

A monsoon rain moves through Guangzhou, flooding the streets and turning the sky a flat gray with low visibility. The balcony at my uncle and aunt's house is covered in an inch of water, their pet turtle in a large ceramic tank on the balcony still stoic and unmoving in the downpour. We've been cooped up inside, and I'm entertaining my aunt with internet memes and pictures of my life in the United States. She's especially amused by photos of me camping and hiking, activities that are just starting to become popular in China, where the "pleasures of wild nature" are brazenly acknowledged as a made-up concept that requires marketing.

My typically easygoing aunt is rankled by the murmurings of a Donald Trump–led trade war. For her, the trade war is *personal*. "Good riddance!" she says. "I say it's good that we have this trade war. We used to export all the good things to the United States and kept all the defective stuff to sell here! And look at how we've damaged our environment, just for you Americans! Crafty people, manufacturing is a dirty job, didn't want to ruin your own country!"

From the Chinese side, it appears that the Americans were cheating the Chinese—American corporations were asking for unimaginably low costs that made it impossible to manufacture high-quality goods, to *not* cut corners. Back in the United States, companies went on to sell these products at astronomical markups, making enormous amounts of money.

As my aunt continues on about the trade war, she starts talking about the quality of goods in her house. She makes me guess how much items in her house cost, as I try to hold back a smirk of amusement in watching a version of *The Price Is Right* unfold before me. "Guess how much I bought this for?" she asks, pointing to a large stuffed animal made out of MCM-patterned leather. She smiles smugly. "It's not about where things are made, but which country does the factory's quality control." She suddenly walks to the kitchen and emerges with a frying pan she purchased in 2012. "Isn't this such good quality? Back when we were all boycotting Japanese goods because of the Diaoyu Islands incident, it was on sale for 80 percent off! It's made in China by a Japanese brand. I had to hide it on the bus, in case anyone noticed that the box had Japanese on it. Someone could have accused me of being a traitor!"

5.

Naomi Wu is a cyborg. On a rainy day, I am scheduled to meet her at the Shenzhen Open Innovation Lab. I am extremely nervous because I want Naomi Wu to like me.

There are Asian women in STEM, and then there's Naomi Wu—she's brilliant, but even more remarkable is her fearlessness in letting her brilliance be admired. Naomi was born human, but she is a self-proclaimed cyborg, a definition made obvious when you watch her videos. She's forthcoming about her cyborg body modifications, including breast implants that light up when she dons a special corset she's designed and built.

Her videos are energetic and witty. Some cover her projects and are instructional, showcasing her engineering prowess to an international audience: a Wi-Fi mini drone inspired by *Neuromancer*; a DIY retro Game Boy kit. Other videos show real-life Shenzhen on the ground, as she visits makerspaces and electronics markets.

While Asian women make up a huge portion of engineering professions in the United States, they are often left out of management and leadership roles. In fact, being Asian creates a *disadvantage* to becoming a leader in tech—Asians are the group least likely to be promoted from individual contributor (i.e., an engineer) to management.[2] This data point should not be taken as a cry of inequity for Asian Americans—it's instead reflective of systemic ways that racial categories work under capitalism in the United States. Asians are presented as soft-spoken, hardworking, and quiet, the "model minority," something that has always sent an alarming message to me: that you can have restricted success if you just comply with the rules, even if the rules are problematic. In a harsher light, these characteristics also signal obedience and acquiescence, characteristics that seem innate to the mindless drone workers I imagined in my uncle's factory.

In the United States, Asians are rarely seen as innovative. Because, after all, to be innovative is to be bold, daring, and brash. Within popular tech discourse, these qualities are more often ascribed to Western white men—heroic inventors with astonishing capacities, like John Galt from *Atlas Shrugged*. The more time I spend with Naomi, I realize: How often is it that a person of color is said to be innovating? How often in the United States do we hear about any other country innovating, especially a non-Western country?

In person, Naomi is down-to-earth and just as energetic as in her videos. She's taller than I expected. Her humility is startling—even though she has hundreds of videos with numerous original projects, she still refers to herself as a DIY tech enthusiast.

And I am struck by her relationship to machines, and to her own body. In the same way hardware can have different enclosures, she says, she sees her own body as an enclosure. She performs body modification because she believes "you have to give the computer what it wants." She anticipates a world of computer vision algorithms on video platforms that increase rankings based on the content of the video, with platforms placing "attractive women" first in search results. Naomi wants to show up first. In an ideal universe, she says, she would have a shop at Huaqiangbei, the famed electronics market of Shenzhen, known as "the market of the future." She would sell body parts, just like computer cases. Want a better arm? Ask her. A different set of eyes? She's got the hookup.

Sitting with Naomi in the Shenzhen Open Innovation Lab, a makerspace full of soldering irons and electrical wires, there's a clear irony. Naomi grew up in Shenzhen. And while many of her classmates, the women she grew up with, now solder in factories, Naomi is soldering in internet videos. While her classmates are seen as mindless drones, she's heralded as a forward-thinking, DIY "maker," part of a broader hacker movement that emphasizes innovation and STEM education.

For a long time, Shenzhen was where so many of America's most innovative products were built, and these products were made by the women Naomi grew up with. It is also the place that popularized *shanzhai*—originally a derogatory Cantonese term for knockoffs or pirated goods. The word "*shanzhai*," directly translated, means "mountain stronghold"—since people from rural mountain villages couldn't afford real Louis Vuitton or officially produced DVDs of *Friends*, the *shanzhai* versions came from low-end, poorly run pirate factories. These *shanzhai* products remain proof to the West that China cannot innovate, it can only copy.

David Li, the founder of Shenzhen Open Innovation Lab, along with the scholar Silvia Lindtner, is bringing this idea of *shanzhai* as imitation into question. They have been researching the innovation ecosystem for the past few years, and they propose the term "new *shanzhai*." David explained to me that part of the original *shanzhai* economy began with copying DVDs. Since copied DVDs couldn't be played by brand-name players, a whole set of products were created to support the copied DVDs. From there, a wildly creative ecosystem appeared.

New *shanzhai* is open source on hyperspeed, an unapologetic confrontation with Western ideas of intellectual property. The designers and engineers of new *shanzhai* products build on each other's work, co-opting, repurposing, and remixing in a decentralized way. At Huaqiangbei electronics market, where Naomi wants her body-parts stall, companies compete and cooperate with one another in a fast-paced dance. Wandering through the stalls of the market, you'll find everything imaginable for sale, and many things you never imagined: holograph generators, 3D printers, karaoke mics with speakers built in, laser cutters, simple cell phones with modular, replaceable parts that require little equipment to open and repair (the opposite of an iPhone).

Shanzhai's past has connotations of knockoff iPhones. New *shanzhai* stands in stark contrast to the increasingly proprietary nature of American technology, pushing us to think about access, maintenance, and the conflation of intellectual property and *civility*. After all, intellectual property rights are not intrinsic. They were created in eighteenth-century England, and tied into the idea of ownership as defining existence—the right to own as the right to be human.[3] And in a time when American corporations are threatening university students researching new technologies with patent lawsuits, *shanzhai* feels more urgent than ever.

Outside the well-funded confines of places like Silicon Valley, for the rest of the world that can't afford US$400 3D-modeling software or US$300 phones that can be repaired only by experts, *shanzhai* is desperately needed. How can you even begin to innovate if you can't afford the tools needed for innovation?

Shanzhai holds the power to decolonize technology. For so long, technology expertise was held by a small circle, a technical elite. "Technology transfer" is the process that many development experts describe, the seeding of tech products, software, assistance, and advice from the metropolitan United States to places like China, Kenya, and even rural America. These projects have had mixed success, often leaving communities dependent on proprietary technology. But in order for technology absorption to happen, such places need the ecosystem, tools, and knowledge to begin to create their own products, tailored to their contexts. *Shanzhai* pushes the boundaries of what we currently think of as innovation and argues for the right not only to use a device or software but also to collaboratively alter, change, and reclaim it—a *shanzhai* economy instead of an innovation economy.

6.

Four hours outside of Guangzhou, in Yangguang village, a group of farmers have formed an organic rice cooperative. The process is not only a *shanzhai* economy in action, but also points to the ways *shanzhai* practices can build a startlingly different world.

The members of Rice Harmony Cooperative pick me up from the long-distance bus station in the nearest town. This part of Guangdong Province is peaceful, the bus station still a single hall. A woman stands looking bored near a defunct X-ray machine. At this bus station, strangely, there's no scanning of personal ID to even enter the station—people leisurely come and go.

We drive to a nearby town for lunch. The restaurant is simple, with battered wooden tables and a glass lazy Susan in the middle. The food is delicious: bright green stir-fried snap peas and preserved pork, vegetable-stuffed tofu, and chewy, perfectly cooked rice. The group's surliest, oldest member, Farmer Qiu, is sixty and an experienced rice farmer. Another, Xinghai, is thirty-three years old, and after years of living and working as a migrant laborer in Guangzhou, he's back in Yangguang village.

Rice in Guangdong has a bad reputation. In 2007, it was discovered that 70 percent of Guangdong rice had unexpectedly high cadmium levels, due to fertilizer overuse. Yangguang village's soil was fortunately unaffected. Still, a few years ago Farmer Qiu sensed that something else was wrong with the soil—it had become hardened and compact, vastly different from the soil he knew from childhood.

Rice farming is a labor-intensive art. Some regions in China rely on methods that are ancient. The rice-fish-duck system, for example, is a dynamic living system that requires no chemical fertilizers or pesticides. The system uses fish that live in the flooded paddies eating insects as a natural insect repellent. Ducks also live in the paddies, providing fertilizer and an added repellent, against snails. During harvest season, the paddies are drained and the fish are easily caught and preserved in wine. The ducks live on for the next season. Paddies are also often small, given the geography of the mountainous rice-growing regions in southern China. Mechanization is difficult.

Rice Harmony's form of organic rice farming ensures that the fate of one person is tied to everyone else's. In Yangguang rice terraces, water moves through ancient paddies from the top of the mountain slowly down to the lowest terraces, in a form of natural irrigation. Every five years, farmers switch paddies through a lottery system, ensuring that no family is stuck with a paddy in a lower or higher region forever. No one has contiguous paddies from this random lottery system, making irrigation a space of constant negotiation. If your paddy is at the top of the mountain and you use up all the water by building a dam, you risk blocking water to your own paddy somewhere else, and also other families'. If you use pesticides in your paddy, residue will flow down into other paddies.

Any change in one rice paddy affects another. Even spraying weeds along the sides of paddies can affect the testing of a neighbor's site. Village meetings happen on account of this pesticide-free, organic rice-farming system. Xinghai shows me pictures from a recent meeting where farmers sat together, debating what to do about all the weeds, taking votes, estimating their yield and harvest for the season. As a cooperative, they all have a fiscal stake in the venture.

Membership in the Rice Harmony Cooperative has been growing every year, and this is no small feat in modern China, where individualism is increasing and the memory of previously disastrous attempts at collectivization by the government remains. Yet the cooperative structure centers the community as the locus of decision-making, creating a collective investment that is resilient under the strain of strong personalities and politics. This is not an easy process to navigate, with cooperative members needing to resolve conflict rather than walk away from it. As a *shanzhai* endeavor, actions cannot be singular and individual. Xinghai and Qiu spend planting seasons in their own fields, and alongside other farmers, providing technical advice and negotiating interpersonal conflict.

Small customized agricultural machines that lift and turn the soil in a special motion are shared among cooperative members. These machines have been built by Qiu and Xinghai, who worked with local blacksmiths to dice up existing machines, creating new blades and attachments. In front of the Rice Harmony lending library are two of these Frankenstein machines.

While Rice Harmony makes its own machines, and uses a range of social media and platforms to sell its rice, people, not technology, stand firmly at the helm of decision-making. It's also an open process—during harvest seasons, Rice Harmony encourages visitors from all over the world to come to learn about organic farming. This type of farming, like any system, is not without its critics, who argue that it can't scale up, it can't create enough yield, that it's not scientific like more engineered, industrial practices. Unsurprisingly, it is the local government that pushes scientific, rational forms of management, including the use of pesticides and fertilizers. Yet for all the debate on process, in Yangguang village, this farming is working.

Rice Harmony serves as a reminder of the humility in innovation, its ability to renew, to change political and social structures. Innovation is literally an ecosystem for Rice Harmony—an ecosystem that does not scale across thousands or millions of users but across the spectrum of time instead, regenerating the soil and community ties from one planting season to the next. For that, you don't need VC funding, a legion of engineers, or millions of users.

I wander through the paddies, past the Frankenstein machines, past the piles of rice straw used as organic fertilizer. If innovation casts the spell of capitalism, in this mountain stronghold, I see *shanzhai* as a verb, used to cast a different kind of spell. To *shanzhai*. To turn protocols into practices that bind us together rather than centralize authority. To turn back the worship of scale and renew our commitments to care. I think back to the words I heard when I was a kid, the other magical phrase, *Made in China*, and the dismissive tone in the man's voice. Barometers of success and innovation are invented by those with money, turning engagement into the surface-level interactions of informed users, rather than the deeper actions that tackle structural, social change by invested citizens willing to hold long village meetings. Entire entrepreneurship programs exist, funded by VCs, designed to foster what VCs see as the core values of innovation. Instead of continuing to accept success and innovation as empty containers, I propose new measures, understanding our world through *shanzhai*, through the ability to care, maintain, renew, and deepen commitments.

I walk by a woman balancing a bucket on her head, off to feed chickens that help control pests. She whistles on her way up a mountain. A whole socioeconomic ecosystem stems from the technical farming infrastructure in this village. It makes me wonder what the parallel might be for our network infrastructure. And as scary as it might sound, to *shanzhai* the world will take time, as we confront our definitions of rationality, as we question intellectual property and what it means to exist meaningfully without boundaries of individual ownership. To *shanzhai* means we give up parts of our ego, rather than innovating a quick fix that scales to millions. After all, money and seed funds are finite, but time is long and ever passing, leaving us with more questions than answers.

·6·

"No One Can Predict the Future"

1.

The police station in Guiyang is loud. The police officers are rowdy, joking and drinking tea while one of them manages to take a nap behind the reception desk. There's a constant stream of people walking in and out, the scent of hot dogs and canned meat wafting through the hallway. Fluorescent lights beam across formerly white tiles, now muddy from Guiyang's incessant construction. At one point, a haggard man in a leather jacket walks downstairs, smelling strongly of body odor and urine, looking confused and disoriented. No one pays him any attention. An ashen whiteboard on wheels sits hastily wedged in the stairwell on the first floor, displaying a list: "Drug cases" says the heading, with five names scrawled in faded marker.

My host, a police officer named Xiaoli, apologizes for the scene—he explains that it is usually like this; they have a lot going on, and it's probably not like the nice, clean police stations I'm used to in the coastal cities of Beijing and Guangzhou. Xiaoli has been touted by media outlets as the handsome millennial police officer of Guiyang, technologically savvy and ready to change how policing is done in the city. I'm meeting with him about the city's Shi You Ren Kou Ping Tai (实有人口平台), or Real Population Platform, which is supposed to be a massive compendium of data on citizens in parts of Guiyang.

The Real Population Platform is one of the products made by Huacheng Technology Company. The platform makes hefty promises of what the company terms "total population control." Biometric data from face scans, state-issued personal identification numbers, fingerprints, and criminal records all come together on the Real Population Platform. Similar platforms have been rolled out across other cities, from Shanghai to Liaoning, although the roll-out is highly fragmented across provinces: some places have more success than others.

The focus of Guiyang's "total population control" is not the entire city population but the urban villages (*chengzhongcun*, 城中村). These areas of the city exist as remarkable and unavoidable reminders of China's urbanization project, and the never-ending process of building (and rebuilding). They thrive freely in big cities until the city government decides to eradicate them. During the winter of 2009, while Beijing's urban villages still existed, I visited one that was adjacent to Yuan Ming Yuan, or the Old Summer Palace. It teemed with life, and poverty—kids playing badminton in the streets, piles of trash, stray dogs sniffing around, and hunks of meat hung to cure outside the entrance of a public restroom by someone taking advantage of scarce outdoor space. It was a rare affordable haven for migrants to the city who could not pay Beijing's astronomical rents.

Urban villages help alleviate the housing burden on

new migrants, yet they are disappearing in a phenomenon not specific to China—the push toward "making places nicer and safer." *Chengzhongcun* directly translated means "village within the city," and these form as Chinese cities expand into or start to surround neighboring farmland. Eventually, the land is cleared for new skyscrapers, and the government compensates the farmers with housing and money. In the best scenario, peasants can become well-off landlords in the new cityscape. In the worst case, they end up with compensation so low that they cannot buy a new home.

Like China's food and language, urban villages have an enormous amount of regional variation. What is common across all urban villages is that they are home to those on the fringes of city life—nannies, housekeepers, construction workers, delivery drivers. In Shenzhen, urban villages have played a key part in the city's rise, nurturing new inventors with brash ideas and informal economies. Yet because of the socioeconomic status of the population residing in urban villages, these areas are deemed dangerous by upper-middle-class urbanites. The term that upper-middle-class Chinese people use to describe this population is "low-quality" (*disuzhi*, 低素质). Strangely, the upper-middle class seems to have no qualms about the low-quality population traveling to wealthier parts, watching over their children and cleaning their homes.

Guiyang's status as a tech boomtown is amplified by its dreamy, sci-fi landscape. The highway is only ten years old, but already vines and eucalyptus have crept through underpasses, covering entrance ramps. Tunnels and bridges tumble through the city, layering cars and people on top of buildings and mountains. The explosive economic growth has led to a number of urban villages forming throughout its rickety, twisting streets. Xiaoli's office is on the second floor of the police station, looking out onto the urban village it's responsible for. Blue construction barriers line the streets, dividing half-formed sidewalks and rubble from the bustle of people, scooters, cars, and bicycles. The streets and the houses are coated with a layer of mud.

Xiaoli and I are the same age—something we immediately bond over. "We're both born after 1980, so let's just be direct with each other, none of that official-style speech," he says, referring to the way most politicians in China talk on-screen: with a robotic air to maintain authority. He trained in the police academy after receiving his undergraduate degree in sociology. Guizhou born and raised, he decided to stick around his home province. A number of years ago, he married, and now he and his wife have a five-year-old daughter.

Even though Xiaoli and I are similar in age, it's hard to unlearn my training from all my childhood textbooks and songs: I feel like I should call him Uncle Policeman, an endearing title of respect for authority (*jinchashushu*, 警察叔叔).

The Chinese police system is complex and used to be much more fragmented across cities and provinces, with little national or centralized information. For example, a person from Shandong that I met along my travels had a criminal record of minor offenses: theft, fighting when drunk. He traveled around China freely, but it wasn't until he tried to go to Beijing in 2018 that police prevented him from entering the city, afraid he'd run amok in the country's political capital.

For a long time, China used its own version of community policing: the local neighborhood association—volunteers from the neighborhood, nosy neighbors and gray-haired grannies—was the eyes and ears for police officers. In recent years, the Chinese police have been relying on outside expertise to help modernize training and policing. There have been numerous "learning exchanges" between China and Europe, as well as the United States, where police officers from China visit police departments abroad to see how modern policing is done. Like capitalism and the free market, China's models of policing have been based on U.S. models. Chinese police academy exchange students have ended up at Sam Houston State University in Texas, and the Los Angeles police even proudly tout "Police Diplomacy," citing the number of police exchange visits between China and L.A.

In places that are experiencing rapid development, like Guiyang, the policing focus is on addressing the surge in crime that comes from economic disparity. Swindles and other schemes to make money, robbery, and muggings are the target. Despite official statistics of a "low crime rate," there's also a proliferation of "criminal villages" in China, where residents of an entire village will engage in some kind of criminal activity. Such villages are like Taobao villages (rural villages that produce merchandise for the e-commerce platform Taobao), but instead of households achieving the Chinese Dream through legal means, they draw on illicit tactics ranging from financial scams involving cake delivery to running kidnapping businesses.[1] China's low crime rate is also due to skewed statistics that don't include urban migrant workers, who are the victims and perpetrators of up to 80 percent of urban crime.

Xiaoli pulls up the Real Population Platform and the first page is a gorgeously shot aerial image. It's not a satellite image, but the result of drone photography, put together by the Beijing geographic information systems company SuperMap.

Each house in the image has been assigned an arbitrary number starting from 1. I ask Xiaoli if it's the actual address and he explains, "So, the thing with urban villages in Guiyang is that there are no actual addresses. All of the construction is very informal. A few of the buildings were here to begin with, village buildings on farmland. Those old buildings are still around, and because there's money to be made renting rooms out, landlords are always adding to their buildings. Or constructing new buildings in between existing buildings."

Xiaoli continues, "The whole reason for this platform is because right now, Guiyang is developing fast, with so many migrants. And 80 percent of Guiyang's migrants live in urban villages. And 70 to 80 percent of all Guiyang crime occurs in the urban villages. So what are we supposed to do? That's why we have this platform, we have to register and track everyone. It's for public safety." The migrants he's talking about are the same people I have met in the countryside throughout my travels: young men and women who have left their rural homes in search of economic opportunity. As migrants they are called *liudongrenkou* (流动人口) in Chinese, the "floating population"—a floating population in a floating world.

Xiaoli's office is small and messy. There's a couch, which I am sitting on, and a blanket and pillow in one corner for a quick nap on long shifts. In another corner, folded clean police uniforms are stacked on top of a mini-fridge, next to a teapot and tins of tea. He clicks around some more on the map. Each house is perfectly numbered, some with hyphens like 1-1 or 684-1. When he clicks on the house, a list of residents pops up in a small window. I ask him how the numbers are so precise, in the absence of formal addresses, and how they get the information about the residents.

In my mind, I imagine some sophisticated computer vision tool that looks at the aerial image, calculates the boundary of the house, and then assigns it a number. I imagine that the city has sensors and surveillance cameras to capture how many people leave the house. I also imagine that the surveillance cameras would know the face and personal ID number of each resident, perhaps tracked all the way from their tiny rural village through the numerous cameras I see everywhere—in train stations, at vending machines, on the street.

Instead, this system relies not on automation but on people. Xiaoli clicks around the map some more. "Every police station has numerous police assistants that live in the urban village. They are our eyes and ears. They are embedded in the community and they're the ones who ground-truth the existence of every single house on this aerial image, giving each house a number. And they are the ones who help landlords register on the platform.

People register through WeChat using the mini program." Xiaoli pulls the WeChat app up on his screen, and taps into the mini program section. After tapping one of the registration buttons, a form comes up. The police assistants Xiaoli refers to are ordinary citizens who have deep ties in the urban village and have lived in the community for a long time. They also alert the police officers at this station of incidents that happen in the village.

"But registration is voluntary, there's no way logistically we can force landlords to register everyone. Plus there's also the problem . . ." He pauses and reaches for a thin stapled book that's hidden under a mess of papers on his desk. On the cover are three passport photos: two men and a woman. "There's the problem that some landlords are old, illiterate, or both. They have no clue how to use WeChat to scan and register their tenants. So the police assistants just give them this booklet to fill out and we put all their information in manually."

He glances at another stack of papers near the window. "It takes a really long time. So right now we only have about sixty thousand people registered on this platform, even after a year or so."

All this information sits in a database, a hulking engineering marvel that underpins so much of our modern world. Databases allow people to read, write, update, and destroy data in a fairly dependable way. They also require the people who build databases to form strong opinions about the world and the way it's structured. For example, the attributes of a user on a platform are dictated by columns an engineer defines in the database. Different databases have different logics for the way data must be formatted, which in turn shapes the way we have come to encode the world. In the case of Real Population Platform, Xiaoli tells me the hardest part is data compatibility.

"To be honest, many of the recent upgrades in Guiyang have been a headache." Xiaoli looks at me, and then suddenly asks, "It is true that Americans each have a number that allows them to be tracked? But that there is only one database that has that number? The social benefits number?" It takes me a second to realize that he means social security numbers. After all, it's not immediately obvious to me that a social security number tracks us. But it does, as any American can attest to: the social security number and credit score follows us, it dictates if we get loans, if we can access credit, and if we can access housing. And while we give our social security number out somewhat casually, research has shown the ways credit scores, attached to our social security numbers, exacerbate deeply entrenched inequality in the United States. For an individual, it's an innocuous number, but on a large scale, it forms a hulking system.

I nod and tell Xiaoli that it is just one number, the social security number, and some private credit-scoring bureaus. Xiaoli looks quizzical. "Well, it's been extra difficult because in China, we have multiple databases. You can use your ID number and one address for work papers, while using a different address for your electricity bill. Especially for migrant workers, it's hard for anyone to tell where you actually live. No one has a permanent address. Before the Real Population Platform, we used a database where the data format was very strict. Each person could only have one address. Duplicated names were not allowed. The Real Population Platform works a lot better, and we have a database where one person can have multiple addresses. Still, trying to reconcile all the entries is difficult. A lot of people have the same names, you know?"

On his screen, he continues to click around. Each entry for an individual has their address, date of birth, and national ID number. Some of the entries have photos, others do not. I imagine a horrible scenario where a case of mistaken identity arises from a database error, a typo, or a dropped row.

For Xiaoli, the difficulties of creating data emphasize not only how important data is but how it doesn't just appear out of thin air, extracted by technology. Data needs to be collected, chased down, massaged, tidied. Which means that the collection of data and the design of a database are intentional: the dimensions of data that need to be collected, defined by a database, already imbue a vision of how a world should be turned granular. Like the translating of a human life into columns and rows, any image of an object is simply a representation of the object. No matter what you use to photograph an object, the image remains a grainy approximation.

I ask Xiaoli when they will be done collecting data on everyone. Xiaoli responds that they are trying to work as fast as they can, but they will never be sure if they have everyone in the database. "We rely on the landlords, because we think a landlord would only like to rent to dependable people. But you never know. We have community police assistants that visit apartments during the day and at night. Many of the migrant workers do jobs that have night shifts. It's hard to tell how many people live in a place. There's some places crowded with bunk beds that allow double the capacity. Night workers sleep in the beds during the day, day workers sleep in the same beds at night."

To collect more data, the local government has been partnering with companies like China Unicom, the mobile carrier, to advertise the advantages of registering on the Real Population Platform. When I ask why China Unicom would push such a campaign, Xiaoli remarks in a cynical, disaffected tone, "Because the more people you have using the platform, the more data people burn. Unicom can make money."

After an hour of me questioning Xiaoli, and several cups of tea, we start talking about his family life and his time working at the police station. He's optimistic about the state of policing, and feels strongly that the community in the urban village is best suited to guide policing strategies. We talk about how he's a young police officer, which he admits hasn't been easy. Many of the older police officers have their own views about how things have traditionally been done and how things should *continue* to be done. He makes a joke about these older police officers being ancient rocks. "You kick them a little bit, and they move an inch. Not a foot, but an inch. I guess you just keep kicking!" Xiaoli adds that older police officers tend to view the technology as an annoyance, but since they have to use it, they will resort to a kind of magical thinking about it, convinced that technology can do more than it actually does, or they eschew deeper understanding for lazy, one-click solutions.

As for the future of Real Population Platform, I wonder if everyone will be as realistic and understanding of what technology can and cannot do as Xiaoli. He has brought up issues before with the platform builders about the user interface, adding certain columns into the database, but has been met with pushback by the engineers. So Xiaoli comes up with his own work-arounds.

Finally, I blurt out, "What about predictive policing?"

Xiaoli handles this question smoothly, laughing at me. "Listen, if we could actually prevent crime, that would mean I found a way to predict the future. None of us can predict the future. If someone wants to commit a crime, they will commit it. But with this platform, we will try to collect the best data sources, and then, with all that data, we can check up on people and know existing areas where crime has happened, who has committed it, and who we should watch out for. For example, we want to figure out who is making homemade drugs in this urban village. We are trying to get electricity usage per household, and sudden spikes in the electricity meter would likely indicate illicit activity. But there are strict data-sharing laws across organizations, so it's not so easy. Even then, there's the question of reconciling all that data, making it useful."

Xiaoli's job is simultaneously chaotic and mundane. Over the course of our entire conversation, phone calls come in, and he scribbles down numbers and addresses. Much of modernizing the police department, becoming more "United States–like," is the emphasis on reporting, tallying, measuring the impact of policing itself. The reasoning is that left without performance indicators and statistics, policing becomes a haphazard endeavor. So to modernize, you get the Real Population Platform and the database, every movement and interaction between the police and a suspect tracked.

Through the computer screen, Xiaoli types in ID numbers, finding people. On-screen, everyone is just another entry in the database. It's when he gets called into the neighborhood that these abstract numbers become animated with emotion: a domestic disturbance between a man and a woman, a belligerent man threatening his cousin. Xiaoli says he tries his best to stay calm. But it's in the gulf between that number in the database and the visceral, adrenaline rush of responding to a call that fear comes in, a gulf created by the abstraction of numbers.

2.

The Megvii (Face++) office in Beijing is boring, banal. It reminds me of many offices in the Bay Area. A beverage fridge sits in the corner, filled with tea instead of LaCroix cans.

After the B or C stage of funding in the startup world, life in the office is marked by a level of nervous comfort. Making software is expensive. It requires engineers, whose market-rate salary is high, whether it's New York, Beijing, or Shanghai. On top of labor costs is the careful massaging of "office vibes," creating a space that's productive but casual, designed to attract talent. There are also constant server costs—computation time can become expensive. On top of that, building certain products involves a long research-and-development phase; it may be years before any customers actually appear. The strangeness of the market and the cost of building software makes it an endeavor bankrolled by a slew of VCs who bring buckets of money, then show up in the office for quarterly meetings, for assurances that their wealth is being well spent.

As an engineer, or "individual contributor," your days are filled with caffeine and snacks, computer screens, and work that alternates between a technical challenge that makes your soul tremble, and unsatisfying procedural tasks. Whatever task you are working on is just a small piece of a bigger picture. It can be difficult to understand the full technical scope of any project, untangling years of code written by someone else who has long since left the company. During my stint as an engineer, working in a San Francisco office, I would sporadically change my text editor to have a custom set of colors, or create new aliases for bash commands—as if variegating my visual landscape would knock me out of a daze. I felt a visceral pleasure in building and optimizing systems. Untangling bugs gave me a surge of adrenaline, like I was a private investigator. Yet coding for work meant placing an emphasis on details. Minutiae can take on significance—maybe a respite, or a natural reaction to inject coding with a touch of sentiment.

At Megvii, engineers sit on one side of the room, some at standing desks, pointing to lines of code on each other's screens. A few have two screens set up, typing into a text editor while idly browsing a shopping site on another screen. Most of the engineers are men, somewhere between the ages of twenty and thirty-five, bespectacled and wearing untucked T-shirts. Sitting among them are some designers, who stare at mock-ups of interfaces. At the other end of the office are what I presume to be the sales and marketing teams. A bored man at the front desk collects packages from the couriers who walk through a set of jumpy automatic glass doors.

If the military science lab was seen as the birthplace of twentieth-century nuclear annihilation, the twenty-first century's death by ecological destruction and unfettered capitalism is symbolized by a glass-cube conference room with a whiteboard. Down the hall, a large product showroom proudly heralds Face++'s achievements. This is a tech company that could be any tech company in the world. This generic geography allays my apprehensions about a Chinese surveillance state. It's instead overshadowed by worry over the making of a global surveillance industry, by people who stand to profit heavily from it.

Face++ is powering many platforms with its facial- and image-recognition algorithms. To be clear, it stores no data on any of its servers—it simply provides the mechanism to recognize a face. First, the algorithm has to recognize that there is a face within an image, and perhaps a primary face within an image of multiple faces. It can distinguish eyes from a nose, which is handy for many of China's Meitu photo-beautification apps that allow you to edit someone's image beyond recognition: changing the shape of your lips, adding lipstick and eyeshadow. In a world inundated with social media images, your selfies need to always look good.

Beyond recognizing parts of faces, the algorithm can start to discern characteristics about you, characteristics to classify you—the distance between your eyes, or the width of your chin. These distances are compared to the average set of collected measurements in order to make categorical assumptions about you—whether you're looking happy or sad that day, or even more troubling judgments.

One step after gathering characteristics is facial recognition: taking the image of your face, distilling it down to measurements, and being able to search a database of faces. Face recognition is a system with numerous parts, and each part is the domain of a private company—whether the one that owns the surveillance cameras used, the algorithm, or the computational power rented out on a server.

The Face++ showroom has plush white carpeting and shiny white walls with inset screens. One wall features real-time camera footage from outside the showroom, in the office and outside the building. The display showcases how fast and precise Face++ computer vision algorithms are—as someone walks by the building, the algorithm detects their blue pants and umbrella. There's also a hidden camera that you can stand in front of and the algorithm instantly classifies your age and gender. I am for some reason characterized by the Face++ algorithm as a twenty-seven-year-old male. The algorithm does not compute my thirty-four-year-old non-binary existence.

Skynet, the unironically named government surveillance system, is also featured in the showroom. The ambitious program hopes to catch China up to the United States in the number of surveillance cameras per person. Under the umbrella of Skynet is the XueLiang or Sharp Eyes program, which implements surveillance in less developed, rural, and autonomous areas like Xinjiang. Although Skynet has nationalist ambitions for a modern surveillance state, the 2018 trade war between the United States and China has highlighted the global nature of the surveillance industry. Cameras used for Skynet are an assembly of parts, with some components coming from as far away as the Netherlands, and chips from the United States. The cameras are assembled in China, some with Chinese firmware.

Megvii/Face++ has investors that span the globe, from South Korea to Russia to Abu Dhabi. Its technical leads have diverse, international educations. When I visit their offices, some of the people I talk to casually mention that they used to live in the United States or worked at *The Wall Street Journal*.

It would have been easy to believe the technological arms race between China and the United States is real, easy to believe that the company behind China's Skynet had an air of Soviet-era secrecy. It would have been easy because at least then a person, a company, a country could serve as the symbol of sinister surveillance. Instead, I was met with a total indifferent openness combined with the dry, surgical threat of a nondisclosure agreement. It didn't just remind me of Silicon Valley; it *was* Silicon Valley.

And in Silicon Valley, money and investment are reliquaries of devotion that allow people to transcend rules. For all the attention the Chinese Great Firewall receives in blocking Twitter and YouTube, Alibaba's Aliyun offers a way to bypass the Great Firewall, for a fee. Other well-known surveillance companies such as Hikvision and SenseTime have a slew of foreign investment. SenseTime's investors include Qualcomm, Fidelity International, Silver Lake Partners (based in Menlo Park, California), and Japan's SoftBank Vision Fund. SoftBank's Vision Fund has ties to Saudi wealth, and spans the globe in its international influence—investing in companies from Alibaba to WeWork and Slack.

In one corner of the Megvii showroom is a display about Meitu, the beauty and cosmetics app with which you can quickly edit your selfies. The commercial is cheerful: a woman gives herself bunny ears, some blush, and lipstick. She makes herself a little paler, her eyes a little bigger, as is the fashion in East Asia—"Caucasian" features are seen as beautiful. These beauty standards, accelerated by convenient beauty app face filters, are evident in the plastic surgery ads that have now overtaken Chinese cities, which feature brown-haired, dewy-skinned white women with the ever-coveted nose bridge.

The commercial runs, with sound effects, on repeat, every minute. Standing in front of the screen, abetted by the occasional coo and glitter effects behind her, the Megvii spokeswoman I talk to makes it very clear: Megvii doesn't store any data, it just makes the algorithm. It is innocent, she says. What governments and companies do with it is up to them. The engineers show up every day and just do their job.

The Megvii algorithms break down bodies and life into numbers, measurements, and parts. This kind of thinking is not new—many of us have been locked into it for hundreds of years, while grasping at an elusive, atomic sense of identity. Looking at the engineers at their desks, it can be easy to judge their ethics, to question why they continue to show up every day when Skynet videos play on loop next door. Yet, like most desk-based jobs these days, the ethical boundary becomes defined by *awareness*. When you have been made accustomed to solving problems by breaking them down into parts, how could you see the larger picture to know whether you're doing harm? The world is certainly complex, but doesn't it feel good helping law enforcement make the world safer? Why *shouldn't* you trust that your work is being used by policy makers who know what they are doing?

3.

In a dark, dingy hallway, I see a flash of bright yellow. My Meituan driver has made it to the twenty-second floor. He has two minutes to drop off my order, and that includes the time it takes to get from the first floor all the way up here. He's running now—past the neighbor's electric scooter leaned against the wall—and does a soaring jeté over the wooden couch in the middle of the hallway, landing with both feet on the floor like a triumphant gymnast. He hands me my bag of cold medicine and wordlessly scurries off.

Meituan is one of the apps that the young analyst in Palo Alto opens multiple times a day. It's an enormously popular delivery app in China, and heralded as one of the latest innovations in China speed, a frenetic pace made possible by complex logistical coordination, the brute force of cheap labor, and the availability of low-cost mobile phones. Gone are the days of riffling through vegetables at the market, batting away old women at the store in a rush for the best produce. Everything from medicine to cooked meals and vegetables can now be delivered to you via Meituan, or scheduled to arrive at your door when you get home from work. Chinese cities are now crowded with an army of yellow-uniformed delivery drivers, riding electric scooters that weave through dense traffic and bike lanes.

As a platform, Meituan's business model is robust. Kai-Fu Lee, founder of Sinovation Ventures, explained what made Meituan so successful at a 2017 talk at the Asia Society in San Francisco. The delivery algorithm is aided by artificial intelligence, specifically machine learning, in crunching the massive amount of location-based geographical data and historical traffic data in order to give the best predictions and driver instructions. Because of China's "gladiator"-like tech scene, competition is tough—Meituan fought hard against Alibaba's Ele.me delivery service. In the end, Meituan prevailed, keeping the cost of each delivery to 70 cents, and placing swap stations for its delivery fleet's electric moped batteries across the city.

A few days after I recover from my cold, I find myself at a Meituan office in the county of Xifeng. It's a funny little town that is still being formed, with buildings piled up out of the grit, clay, and gravel of its lumpy mountain geography. Even the food here has an aftertaste of dust. The town is so small that it's not even big enough yet to be ranked on the city classification scheme.

The Meituan office is located across the sky bridge from a sad-looking piano shop. Inside the office, two electric scooters sit, connected to power strips with tangled wires that lead to batteries and phones. One poster hangs next to a mirror, showcasing the three required styles of dress for Meituan employees: a spring/fall uniform, a short-sleeve summer outfit, and a winter jacket with coat and gloves. Everything is bright yellow. A large poster shows the best couriers for the month in Xifeng, and their awards. First place is Luo Re Ding, who gets an RMB 300 bonus (US$40, the cost of one blockchain chicken); in second place is Wang Yun, with an RMB 200 bonus. Third place gets a battery pack for their cell phone, and fourth place a waterproof cell phone case.

It smells like stale cigarettes, sweaty socks, and takeout food. Plastic cups are strewn everywhere. Four computers sit, each with a mouse pad that shows the happy Meituan mascot—a plump kangaroo. In the corner is an enormous stuffed Meituan kangaroo with worn-out yellow fabric, on top of a pile of branded helmets. Two very nice women, looking bored on their cell phones, run the office. A few heat lamps blast hot dry air into the room, amplifying the smell of stale cigarettes. Welcome to the Xifeng branch of a company that was valued at US$55 billion for its IPO.

I ask the women what exactly they do. They tell me they perform office tasks, dealing with admin duties and customer complaints. There are only about twenty couriers today in the city of Xifeng. Meituan is just getting started here.

On the wall, recruitment flyers are tacked everywhere. The salary breakdown is also posted on the wall. Unlike most gig economy drivers in the United States, Meituan couriers are paid a base salary of RMB 2,000 (US$280) a month. They don't receive any benefits besides accident insurance, so they rely on their government-provided health insurance. Each delivery earns RMB 4 on top of their base salary.

Everything else listed on the salary breakdown sheet is a fine. Being late for a delivery incurs an RMB 5 fine. A bad review costs the driver an RMB 20 fine. Refusing to take an order after it is assigned in the system results in an RMB 100 fine, and being too early for a delivery is a whopping RMB 500 fine. Although the base salary initially seems appealing, the long list of fines creates a precarious existence for the workers. It parallels gig work in the United States—DoorDash drivers and Task-Rabbits. In both cases, the larger system, the platform, off-loaded any operating risk to the workers, allowing the platform to shirk responsibility to customers. Through fee structures of bonuses, fines, and competition to be courier of the month, work is gamified, just like in the United States.

When I ask the two women how long the structure has been like this, one of them shrugs. "I mean, it's been like this ever since we started. But I don't make the rules. I just enforce them. I'm just doing my job."

4.

In 2012, a close friend and I traveled to Baotou in Inner Mongolia, a rare earth processing town. North of the town were the Bayan Obo mines, estimated to have 70 percent of the planet's (known) rare earth deposits. Iron and fluorite surged through the earth. After being excavated, it was processed and shipped out, transported to Baotou, to be turned into cell phones, computers, and batteries.

Inner Mongolia was my friend's home province. The trip was his attempt for us to see the grasslands of the region—instead, it ended up being a tiring journey on buses and trains, a requiem for the last parts of nomadic Mongolian life. We drove from a copper mine to a coal mine outside of Hulunbuir, watching straggly sheep herds in the waning grassland. He's ethnically Mongolian, but his family ended up on the Chinese side of the border during the split between independent Mongolia and Inner Mongolia as a territory of China. As an ethnic minority in China, he has a fraught relationship to the government. Early assimilationist policies, alongside forced resettlement of nomadic Mongolian herders into Han Chinese–built cities, has led to an erasure of Mongolian language and culture in the region. Mining, an industry exalted by the national government, is desecrating pastureland—these tensions were crystallized in a series of 2011 protests after a Han Chinese miner ran over a Mongolian herder.

Carving away the hours while waiting for the next bus out of Baotou, in feverish boredom, we shared stories from the past. My friend flatly revealed that he had, at the age of nineteen, spent several years in prison after he and some childhood friends had a messy entanglement with a local bank. The incident was driven by his naive teenage wish to finally have the fiscal means to leave the dusty backwaters of Inner Mongolia, to escape the empty life that awaited him. The disappearing wild horses and the summer sounds of frogs, the coal mines being excavated, devoid of meaning. Moved by a teenage claustrophobia that I recognized in myself, he and his friends tried to get rich quick.

He recalled the hard labor, the time spent sitting

doing nothing in jail. The occasional taste of a cigarette. The paralysis he felt after he left prison, spending two years watching *shanzhai* Godard movies at his parents' house, in a deep depression. Dreaming of a freedom, a kind of global, cosmopolitan world, dreaming of moving to the United States. Decades later, his life would look remarkably different in Beijing. Yet he still held his criminal record, which authorities saw as adding to his already suspect status as an ethnic minority, a migrant in Beijing. Surveillance would follow him everywhere, someone always keeping track.

In the dusty, obscured orange sun of Baotou's afternoon light, I felt a pang of intimacy. In a socioeconomic system that required deep chasms, my friend said it was unthinkably funny and bizarre to him that the two of us should have ever met. Him, a migrant to Beijing who had barely finished high school, an ex-convict, an ethnic minority in China. Me, a Han Chinese American expat, Harvard educated, a dutiful American citizen and taxpayer, purchaser of cell phones that aided in the creation of dusty backwaters like Baotou, the unspoken reliance on my U.S. passport and the government behind it. It is easy to feel guilty about privilege when it's in the abstract. Instead, I looked at him and took his hand.

In the moment that I should have felt fear toward him, a suspicion that he wanted something from me, I instead felt a strong flash of sadness. He had already recognized how the world might see him from the outside. He lived through the lens of another.

I think of him and his lifelong awareness of being watched. We have a sense of how entangled we are in a culture of surveillance and, especially these days, how that culture proliferates with smart devices like Alexa in our homes, or as we spew clever quips on social media. The awareness of surveillance capitalism grows.

Yet as a tactic of policing, surveillance has always been crucial in *making* criminality throughout history, drawing a line between those on the so-called right and wrong sides of society. And this line drawing is enabled by distilling life into arbitrary parts: class, race, gender, with the line of criminality itself constantly shifting throughout time, serving political-economic crises. "Crime went up; crime came down; we cracked down," writes the scholar Ruth Gilmore.[2]

"I don't mind being surveilled by Alexa because I have nothing to hide" is a refrain I often hear. And while some of us might feel indignant about *corporate* platforms surveilling us, part of our indignation also arises because it wasn't part of the bargain—people on the "right" side of society weren't supposed to be surveilled. Privacy is seen as what we give up for safety, and safety is the freedom from fear.

And in San Francisco, whenever I hear people talk about corporate, profit-driven platforms that track and monetize our data, I nod vigorously. Yet I long for a leap, for us to reconsider how surveillance has been made into a moral imperative in policing, how somehow the police state has been naturalized. Surveillance has *never* just been about crime, as historians and scholars like Simone Browne have shown, and it is in fact deeply tied to race, ethnicity, and white supremacist constructions of criminality. Just as platforms off-load risk onto gig economy workers, unchecked capitalism creates economic inequality and off-loads the risks and fears onto us all.

In order for us to challenge surveillance, we will have to move beyond corporate, profit-driven platforms that track us and monetize our data, but more importantly we will have to combat our own fears and illusions of safety. We must question the culture of surveillance and carceral punishment that condition us to think living with fear is the only way of understanding we are alive. We must rethink what safety means, and what it means to build communities that allow everyone to live an unbounded life, instead of punishing people for being poor.

As the activist Tawana Petty puts it, it's recognizing the difference between "safety" and "security." This work is deeply tied to transformative justice and the work of prison abolition. Until we do this work, we will not be able to move past surveillance as normalized activity and we will not be able to adequately advocate for the right to privacy for all.

I think of my friend and the tired look on his face, the slight look of shame as he disclosed to me his past. We had known each other for a few years, traveled for countless hours. I think of the relief he said he felt after telling me, and him imagining what I would think for our entire time together. His eventual disillusionment with the United States after visiting American cities, where he felt that Americans were not as free as they imagined, but instead governed by fear in their everyday actions.

I don't want to live in a world where privacy is declared a human right only for a category of humans like me, and not for others. And this right to privacy is not an individualistic one of secrets and stories, but a social one that requires us to lead with trust in our daily lives.

In doing so, we might even end up with a freedom from fear, the freedom we are looking for in notions of "safety."

There is another side to data, illuminated once we understand constructions of fear in our day-to-day lives. "Can data ever know who we really are?" asks the policy researcher and activist Zara Rahman.[3] For my friend and many others, the data on a past crime remains committed to his record. And while his life changes—he becomes a friend, a husband, a doting father, an artist, an uncle—all the data points about his past remain static. Data cannot truly represent the full spectrum of life. It remains a thin slice of the world. There is always some kind of bias built in. Yet we imagine numbers to mean something, and this creates a common tendency that the statistician Philip B. Stark calls "quantifauxcation": the attempt to assign numbers or quantify phenomenon, as if quantitative data can offer certainty.[4] Some strategies for quantifauxcation, says Stark, include saying things people *want* to believe, and adding opaque complexity to models, since complexity has become conflated with accuracy.

The mixture of crime data with prediction is the realm of quantifauxcation. Xiaoli admits he can't predict the future, but remains convinced that collecting data about past crimes in the urban village will highlight "problem areas," helping to focus an overloaded police force. Paying extra attention to problem areas raises an observation bias in itself. The more patrols are assigned to a certain area, the more crimes are observed. And really, the numbers don't mean much in themselves, except as markers of both how policing has replaced social welfare services and the corporate-style expectations of efficiency that are put on police officers. Xiaoli's predictive policing reflects the circular logic that has become embedded across many cultures, enabled by technological solutionism. As the scholar-activist Ruha Benjamin puts it, "Crime prediction is better understood as crime production."[5]

The intractability of life to be rendered captive to simple numbers, lines on a record, reaffirms the powerful act of living against the weight of data used toward predictive ends. To shed the belief that data is predictive and powerful is to push away surveillance as necessity. Shedding our devotion to data gives a depth of meaning to presence, carving out new paths and ways of living beyond categorical drop-down menus, checkboxes, and forms.

The data gathered on me is cheap and meaningless, just as the data gathered on you is already meaningless after the moment has passed. My last ten purchases on my credit card do not speak to the poetry of my mornings, the slant of Californian sun at 4:00 p.m., the moment between dream and waking. In a life with specificity and intention, the power of surveillance and data becomes deflated, the industrial quality of rendering people into categories vanishes. The call to an examined life begins. There is no intrinsic value in the categorical. There is nothing to be said about bare existence that gains power through classification.

In 1952, the psychiatrist and philosopher Frantz Fanon advocated for living *against* the weight of history. He was writing during the beginnings of the Cold War, with World War II still a close memory. The reorganization of world powers started to shape fields of economic development and scientific management, as well as decolonization and postcolonial movements. In that time of tumult, questions of what it meant to live, and what it meant to be human, were at the forefront of many people's minds, like Fanon's, as they worked together to build new societies. Living against history can equally be applied to our understanding of data—"I am not a prisoner of history. I should not seek there for the meaning of my destiny. I should constantly remind myself that the real leap consists in introducing invention into existence. In the world through which I travel, I am endlessly creating myself."[6]

I think back to what Xiaoli said to me: "No one can predict the future." And Xiaoli is right. When I see my friend now, holding his chubby six-month-old against his cheek, his son's small round toes curled, I see a joy that transcends any columns in a database, any notes on a record, any human-programmed algorithm. In the world in which we travel, our right to life hinges on our endlessly creating ourselves.

.7.

Gone Shopping in the Mountain Stronghold

1.

The shortest route between the tiny, thousand-year-old village of Shangdiping and the nearest town is a meandering five-kilometer walking path through mountains, rice paddies, and bamboo forest. Over the past thousand years, everything arrived to Shangdiping via this path, hauled by villagers on wooden yokes. Whether it was getting your rice dehusked or going to town for a relative's wedding, you traveled this single mountain path. One rainy winter day, I walk along this ancient trail guided by a hand-drawn paper map, after hearing about Shangdiping from a friend who makes a yearly pilgrimage to this village.

In 2017, another route to Shangdiping was finished—a paved cement road wide enough to fit a single car and motorbike. This cement road signaled a new era for the tiny village, an era of e-commerce and development. A village of subsistence farmers would learn how to become part of the market economy.

The village is home to around nine hundred residents, all of them Dong, an ethnic minority group in China with populations also scattered across Laos and Vietnam. The Dong are known for their "intangible cultural heritage" of polyphonic singing in their Kam-Sui language, their special rice breed, skillful wooden architecture, and indigo dyeing. They have called the mountainous valleys and rice terraces of Guizhou Province home for thousands of years.

In Shangdiping, an old wooden tower sits in the middle of the village square. Wooden beams overlaid with ceramic roof tiles cover a firepit and several benches, a place for village meetings. In the winter, a roaring fire in the center provides warmth and a place to burn village trash, ashes flying through the air. The village has been like this for hundreds of years, originally settled by army fighters searching for a *shanzhai* in its original sense, a mountain stronghold.

Shangdiping is becoming part of the market economy, and its transition is full of magical juxtapositions. Entering the village, I stop to watch a pig being slaughtered along the river, in front of an E-Commerce Help Station that is coated in stickers advertising speedy courier companies: Zhongtong, Shunfeng, Tiantian. The large sow is bucking its front leg, squealing in agony, an eerie humanlike shriek that echoes loudly through the rice terraces. After a few minutes, it's silent. One man nonchalantly blowtorches the pig, while another man, with a cigarette dangling from his mouth, holds a shovel over the pig. He vigorously scrapes the pig to get the burnt hairs off, the motion jiggling the pig's legs back and forth. The knife is still stuck in the pig's chest. School has let out for the day and a dozen kids stream out from a wooden building into the town square, bouncing off the wood-framed buildings with elation. A pudgy young girl watches the pig slaughter. She gives a slow, throaty laugh as if it were the pig's fault for getting killed.

The only restaurant in the village has no signage, but it is simple to find: it's where people in the village square will direct you during lunchtime if it's obvious you're not from Shangdiping. Inside the restaurant, I sit and chat with the owner, Ren Fujiang, as he attempts to fix his Canon printer. Its plastic yellowing, and covered in dust, the battered printer won't cooperate as he repeatedly removes and inserts the cartridge, his hands splattered with black ink. A large, bright red calendar with portraits of Xi Jinping and Hu Jintao is tacked onto the wall. Fujiang is trying to print out the next semester's attendance sheet for the village elementary school. While many rural schools have been closed down for lack of willing teachers, it's encouraging to see that there's still an elementary school in Shangdiping. Fujiang's son, Xiao Niu, tells me that they've had trouble keeping teachers around. Hopefully the new road will help, he says.

The food at this restaurant is humble. The restaurant is actually the first floor of Fujiang's home, and the kitchen is his family kitchen. His son lights up the brick stove in the corner, coal burning underneath a large wok. A small bowl of stir-fried tomato and egg appears, pickled radishes, a few leaves from the season's last cabbage, and rice from their family's harvest. The choices are limited by what Fujiang and his family have grown over the past year and what they've managed to pickle. These tomatoes, the cabbage, and the rice are grown from heirloom seeds, preserved from previous years' crops.

The portions are laughably diminutive compared to

the large plates of food doled out in major cities. Yet the tomatoes are flavorful, the cabbage sweet and crisp. "This is all food we grow for ourselves," Fujiang tells me. "We eat the good stuff—unlike you city people. No pesticides or fertilizer for us, too expensive to use that stuff anyway!" The dishes are heightened by fermented chili paste, which comes from the family's chili plants. It's so good that I ask Fujiang if I can buy some. He pauses, and then says it's fine, but he has no container for me to put the paste in. His son riffles through a cabinet and emerges with a large empty Sprite bottle.

"How much is it?" I ask, and it takes him a minute to think through this. It's clear that in this village, there are no hungry capitalists yet, no price stickers and scales. Finally, he says, "Is RMB 10 (US$1.40) a fair price? Can you pay me via WeChat?"

2.

Shangdiping is just one of many villages that the government hopes to lift out of poverty. Prior to opening the restaurant I eat at, the family had a life defined by subsistence farming. The rural village collective allocated each household enough land to plant, to feed themselves. Depending on weather and luck, the yearly harvest would yield enough food for a year, maybe a little extra if they were lucky. Taking care of the land was an incentive in itself, since it determined how well your crops would grow the next year.

Slowly, through local government policies, other options were created besides the gamble the family took on farming every year. And slowly too, younger generations started leaving the village, like Fujiang's son, Xiao Niu, who is tall, thin, and quiet. He left to do construction work in the city of Guangzhou, bringing extra income back to the family.

Xiao Niu did not stay in Guangzhou. He now helps his family with work in the fields, cooking food for the occasional guest, and, as I glean from his WeChat feed, also helping with village construction projects. When he got back to Shangdiping, he married a local Dong woman. His wife occasionally comes into the house during our meal, her long hair uncut for at least a decade, piled on top of her head and held in place with wooden combs. They have a baby who toddles around the house, strapped into a walker.

Why didn't Xiao Niu stay in Guangzhou? "City life is not designed to keep you there," he says. "If you earn RMB 3,000 or 4,000 a month, that's great money, sure, but city residents spend more than that just on rent. You can't build a life off that." Sometimes we play the game or the game plays us. And so Xiao Niu took the money he'd earned and returned home to the mountains of Guizhou, determined not to be played by the game. It at least was enough money to do things like improve his parents' house and buy his dad a printer.

Part of tackling poverty means being able to measure and map it. There are disputes among experts in the field of international development on how to do this, especially on how to measure poverty in communities that rely on farming. Defining household assets is one method, but with farms, depending on the season when you take the measurements, assets will change before and after harvest season. Another method is quantifying household disposable income—the ability to purchase. It's these on-the-ground variations, compounded into larger macroeconomic figures, that lead to claims that global poverty is getting much better, or much worse. Yet these claims do not answer how people become poor in the first place, and, if we have found the key to eradicating poverty, why it still exists.

However you quantify it, the facts laid bare are these: Shangdiping and other places in rural China have higher infant mortality and lower life expectancy rates than cities. Education access is lower. And the entrenched poverty of China persists in its remote, rural, ethnic minority regions such as Xinjiang, Tibet, Ningxia, Guizhou, and Yunnan.

And so economic experiments are being unveiled as part of Rural Revitalization. These experiments rely on technology and the internet as catalysts, creating new socioeconomic ecosystems of rural entrepreneurship, hearkening back to the Town and Village Enterprises of the 1980s. Such initiatives use e-commerce, mobile payment, and broadband, bolstered by the traditional Chinese art of massive infrastructural projects like roads, walls, and high-speed rail. Accompanying these economic changes is also a shift in rural culture, as the dynamics of the market become interlinked with traditional family dynamics.

These experiments are unfolding across a wild landscape. A patchwork of private corporations and delayed government oversight exists alongside friction between peasant entrepreneurs and local government. More than an isolated experiment in rural China, the rural e-commerce explosion is testament to the interdependence between rural China and the rest of the world, in an age when most of our actual daily labor in cities has become shopping and consuming online.

3.

I tell Xiao Niu about the E-Commerce Help Station and the pig slaughtering. Shangdiping's attempt at e-commerce is going very poorly, he says. He laughs good-naturedly when he says this, as if he doesn't mind telling the truth—something people loathe doing these days, when preserving the image of success is about the same as achieving success.

"We just got the cement road in 2017, and even then, it's a trek! We were supposed to post all our stuff online, on a Taobao store. People in Shanghai ordered some eggs after the road was opened and it took twelve days for the eggs to get to them. Not good if you're just trying to make some dinner," Xiao Niu says.

How do you quantify what could be sold from Shangdiping? I imagine an auditor coming into the village, making a checklist: pristine soil, organic vegetables, clean air. But a viable product is hard. Shipping vegetables requires refrigeration, which in turn requires more money. Fujiang's complaint was that most urbanites didn't even like the organic vegetables—too imperfect, too full of holes. I heard this same sentiment from several organic farmers, including one who sourced to Matilda's Yimishiji platform. The solution in Shangdiping was to sell eggs.

E-commerce or not, Fujiang assured me that the village is going to develop. He pulls out his phone and shows me an illustrated development plan of Shangdiping. While Shangdiping currently has utilitarian stone bridges over the river, the development plan features highly elaborate Dong-style covered bridges, protected from the wind and rain. The village is pursuing a tourism strategy common in China—"cultural tourism," which amps up the cultural capital of being a certified ethnic minority village. It explains the over-the-top performance of Dong culture in this development plan. Guesthouses abound through the village, along with single trees strategically placed by the roads, an odd detail given that Shangdiping is surrounded by forests of pine and ficus trees, punctuated by bamboo.

I had to ask an obvious question: "Last time I was here, I had to use the bathroom and it was a wooden board with a hole in it, placed over the river, a small fence for privacy. Will the development plan address this . . . issue?"

Fujiang laughs. "Yes, yes, we're going to put in a wastewater system for the entire town. After that, it's easy. We've already got broadband internet. Upstairs is our home and there are some extra rooms. We're ready for tourists. Even now you can find us on the internet. Just look up 'Slowly, Slowly Guesthouse and Restaurant.' And let me know when you're coming next. Bring all your friends!"

4.

Thousands of kilometers to the north of Shangdiping, in Shandong Province, the bathroom in Dinglou village is nearly glamorous, except for one design flaw: it is entirely transparent. Where walls should be, there are instead glass panes, showcasing your personal bathroom time as if you were onstage. Saddled with new wealth, the proprietors of the China Number One Taobao Village Hotel have opted for an elaborate interior design scheme that seems to scream *CITY! LIGHTS! GLAMOR!* The marble stairs from the lobby are narrow and dark, with a few slanted steps, but upstairs the hallway has deep blue lights—reminiscent of a derelict strip club or a Gaspar Noé film.

I'm here with a cinematographer and a director to shoot a movie on tech in China. We're all sweaty and exhausted after twelve hours of filming. That night, our cinematographer is visited by a ghost.

When we reconvene the next morning, he tells us about it—it was a loud ghost yelling in Shandong dialect, trying to get a cigarette. "But all I've got is this e-cigarette," our cinematographer replied. Annoyed, the ghost left the room, skulking back to where it was buried, across the street.

Dinglou village is a successful e-commerce town, tucked into the flat, dusty plains of Shandong. Its success shows in the restaurants, the paved roads, the bustling morning market, and even the village ghosts who have become rich enough to pick up smoking. The daily open-air market is a veritable bazaar of wonders, but the main highlight might be a man selling sesame oil out of an enormous wok the size of a small adult. Dinglou and its neighboring town, Daji, are unusually wealthy for villages in rural China. Dinglou is filled with these market spectacles, which go beyond typical rural open-air markets of vegetables and garlic. There is even a bakery that sells cakes with RMB 100 bills embedded in the frosting. The village boasts about its broadband fiber-optic cable, purportedly faster than internet in Shanghai. It's a boomtown here, and it's miserable.

At the Rural Internet Center, a short beige building located next to a swath of fields, an exhibit tells the fabled origin story of Dinglou's success. An attendant hands each of us a bottle of lukewarm water as we stand in front of a large LCD screen. He turns on a video. The video's sound blasts through large, cheap speakers placed throughout the exhibition hall, tiled in Taobao.com's signature orange. "Rural Taobao is the future!" the narrator's voice booms through the speakers.

In rural Taobao land, there is no government, just the rules of Taobao. Alibaba makes a range of platforms, including 1688.com (the digits when said out loud in Chinese sound like "Alibaba"), a domestic site for bulk purchases. But Alibaba is most well-known for Taobao .com, a huge e-commerce site that allows small businesses and individuals to sell directly to consumers. All the goods are new, and some of them are homemade. As of 2017, Taobao had six hundred million monthly active users, compared to Amazon's three hundred million monthly active users. Everything, and I mean everything, can be found on Taobao: a gold-plated lighter in the shape of people in coitus that moans when you ignite it, umbrellas in an array of animal shapes and decorations, red dates the size of eggs, tea, fried-dough fritters, banned books, banned video games, and Adidas Yeezy shoes that range from obviously fake to high-quality fake ("AAA level" in knockoff lingo) to very much real.

The video we're watching on how rural Taobao is the future flashes, spins, whirs in a thicket of video effects that look like they came from a Microsoft PowerPoint presentation circa 1990. The narrator describes how in 2013 the internet giant Alibaba launched the Rural Taobao strategy, aimed at improving the lives of those in rural China. It's as if Google decided to turn itself into a branch of the United Nations, or as if Amazon decided it suddenly wanted to offer assistance to an Appalachian coal-mining town by helping its citizens start candy businesses and giving them Amazon-backed loans.

The strategy is two-pronged: Rural Taobao and Taobao villages. The first involves a series of Rural Taobao Service Centers, which are usually located at the village convenience stores and revolve around one URL: cun.taobao .com. At these Rural Taobao Service Centers, Taobao contracts with one or two local villagers as brand ambassadors. These brand ambassadors are not directly employed by Alibaba but are paid a small amount to help villagers buy and select items, as well as access other services from the e-commerce platform, such as buying train tickets online and scheduling doctor's appointments. Shopping is the main highlight of rural Taobao, but digital literacy is also emphasized. In the rural Taobao world, "digital" means anything Alibaba-related. Villagers may not be buying gold lighters anytime soon, but practical goods like laundry detergent and long underwear are popular with rural users on the site. Other companies have followed suit with this rural user acquisition strategy: companies from JD.com to Pinduoduo (an e-commerce app that had a US$1.6 billion IPO on NASDAQ) have flooded rural users with an assortment of marketplaces that sell various knockoff, *shanzhai* brands that cater to the rural income bracket. Scrolling through Pinduoduo, one finds a bizarro land of gonzo-capitalism, with PUMPERS diapers, SHAP TVs, and New Bunren sneakers.

To spend money, you need money. This is the ambitious part of the Alibaba Rural Taobao Strategy: rural economic growth. It involves planting the seeds for a Taobao village. A Taobao village is a place where more than 10 percent of the village households are manufacturing at home for Taobao.com. To accomplish this, Alibaba has a whole branch of its company focused on rural development, rural finance, and rural Taobao. It also has its own rural research institute, AliResearch, which examines the business cycles of Taobao villages to understand their successes and failures.

Dinglou was officially designated by Alibaba in 2012 as the first Taobao village. Since then, the number of Taobao villages has soared from 1,311 in 2016 to 3,202 across twenty-four provinces in China in 2018. When I talked to one researcher at AliResearch, he was hopeful that the number would grow. After all, it's a win-win model for Alibaba and economists in the central government. It repopulates the countryside and addresses the "hollowed-out village" phenomenon. Young people who leave places like Dinglou village find themselves coming back home instead of staying in cities. One official document from Dinglou boasts that five hundred college students have returned home because of the thriving e-commerce, which is a population boom for a village. It brings talent and knowledge back to the countryside, and ensures that the countryside will also develop, instead of growth concentrating in cities.

And when the villagers aren't producing goods for Taobao? They still continue to farm their fields. It's a version of the gig economy, though I can't quite tell if the farming or the manufacturing is on-demand.

The production focus of Dinglou is on costumes used for stage and film. Over 90 percent of villagers help produce these costumes in some way. We walk through the exhibition hall of the Rural Internet Center. The costume display is eerie, with mannequins that look like they might come alive any second. Elaborate headdresses on top of a Monkey King costume, a plastic mask with two dark holes for eyes. Red puffy gowns for wedding photographs on a mannequin with plastic blond hair sculpted into a flapper bob. A series of animal costumes for small children, for school plays. Santa Claus costumes and a version of a princess that hints at Snow White without totally violating copyright, seven small mannequins behind her that appear to be either children or dwarfs. Army uniforms from all over the world, which upon closer inspection have falling-apart seams, for theater plays and films.

As I walk through the hall, sipping my lukewarm

water in the weak air-conditioning, I'm reminded of similar exhibition halls that I've seen in Inner Mongolia that herald the joys of rare earth mining and cashmere production. Rural areas have been sites of extraction, conveniently located out of sight for urbanites. Yet in an age when we are shifting to a "digital economy," when much of our lives revolves around shopping, desiring, and performing for an unknown public online, the existence of a place like Dinglou, making stage costumes, seems to be the obvious, ironic progression.

Rising rents in cities have also pushed factory manufacturing costs up in China, making goods less competitively priced. In the countryside, where rural residents are entitled to land by their *hukou*, where rent and labor costs are low, the geography of Taobao villages becomes a competitive advantage. This "spatial fix" is something other companies, like Foxconn, are also turning to in a more centralized way, setting up a factory in rural Henan instead of in expensive, urban Shenzhen. It's no wonder the Rural Revitalization document of the Chinese Communist Party is exuberantly betting on e-commerce. The internet promised disembodiment, but the internet has never been more material. The notion of discrete physical and digital worlds is nothing but a convenient fiction.

5.

It's Saturday and the screen-printing shop in Dinglou is still hard at work. Banners line the streets of Dinglou and Daji saying, NOTHING BEATS COMING BACK TO YOUR HOMETOWN

TO RUN A TAOBAO BUSINESS! The air is hazy, yellow, and dry. Families manufacture costumes during peak seasons like Christmas and Halloween, and during the agricultural planting season they tend to their fields. In the meantime, a whole industry to support costume making has sprouted up in the village, and everyone's hard at work on costumes during the summer, once the fields have been planted.

The screen-printing shop is just one of many storefronts along a large main street. Embroidery businesses sit next to open fields, with the loud clattering of needles as machines churn out intricate designs, controlled by computers. One street is bumpy, uneven, and filled with large craters. A man is outside torching a rubbery substance, a blast of hot air in the already steaming summer heat. In one family workshop, a wife comes downstairs from the family's living space to the manufacturing area—the epitome of a startup garage. She outlines patterns onto a thick slab, hundreds of sheets of fabric stacked on top of each other. After she's done drawing the pattern, she hops up on the table in her kitten-heel shoes and red skirt, without protective eyewear or earplugs. Her husband pulls out a jigsaw, clamps the sheets of fabric to the table, and hands the jigsaw to his wife. She starts cutting through the fabric slab. Her hand is steady as she pushes the jigsaw along the pattern lines. Next to the table is her mother-in-law, who watches, helping affix labels onto packages. After the woman is finished, a couple hundred precut pieces are ready to be sewn and dyed into stage-play army uniforms. Outside, the sound of their dog barking echoes above the buzzing machine noises. A lone chicken squawks.

6.

Ren Qingsheng, the e-commerce pioneer of Dinglou, types with two fingers. He uses his left and right pointer fingers to hunt and peck at the keyboard, vigorously, with a confident clack. His hands are darkened by the sun, rough and calloused. Although he's a millionaire success story in the village, featured in the Rural Internet Center and also recently elected village party secretary, he's still often out in the fields, working as part of the village environmental commission. He's in the office today, running back and forth between the town hall and his family's workshop, which is also his home, and which sits in front of his family's agricultural fields.

Most Chinese villages have a set of loudspeakers, strapped to electricity poles, for village announcements. In the morning, as village party secretary, Ren Qingsheng heads toward the village headquarters, a small brick building. Inside the headquarters, tacked to the wall, is a paper Communist Party flag that's discolored orange from sunlight. Below the flag, in cartoonish font, is a slogan: DEAR, DID YOU TAOBAO TODAY?

He turns on the village PA system with a piece of paper in hand and does the daily announcement. "Fellow comrades, villagers . . . as you know, we need to get rid of these poplar trees. We must cut them down. We are a proud village. I advise you to cut down the trees. I did it last year and I had more room to plant vegetables. If you love trees, you could replace the poplar trees with fruit trees. Please ask us for advice."

In 2009, Ren Qingsheng and his wife decided to start

an e-commerce shop, despite lacking business experience or a computer. "The whole thing was actually my wife's idea," he explains in his office, overlooking a stack of receipts. "My wife worked as a manual laborer at a nearby sand manufacturing plant. It was really hard work and took a toll on her body. She had to retire early because of the physical toll it took. At home, we weren't sure how we were going to make ends meet. You have to understand, planting the fields only yields an income of RMB 5,000 a year, if you're lucky. And we have two children to send to school."

He pauses. "My wife is educated for a peasant, she went to vocational high school. I have an elementary school education. So she's much more open to new things than I am. At the time, there was a couple in Dinglou who had been making these costumes for photography studios at home—simple costumes. They would travel around the county on bicycle selling these costumes, because at the time no one had enough money to buy a car. And my wife came up with this idea, she had heard about Taobao from a relative of hers. So she thought, let's try selling costumes on Taobao."

To start off their Taobao shop, Ren and his wife borrowed the hefty sum of RMB 1,400 from a family member, to buy their computer. Posting items on Taobao.com was a learning curve for Ren—Chinese characters are input via pinyin, the system of romanization. Ren had to borrow his daughter's elementary school textbook for the task, since he had dropped out of school before learning pinyin.

After a few months, Ren and his wife received their first order. "At the time, we didn't know anything about online banking. We had to send out the costumes, and I was so nervous. Every day I would go all the way to the bank and check our bank account. And the money did come! My wife and I immediately went out and bought a whole chicken to slaughter in celebration."

After this first order, Ren slowly got the hang of online selling and the online payment system, Alipay. Alipay itself got easier and easier to use, morphing into the e-payment, bank transfer, peer-to-peer payment system, and wealth management app it is today.

Over the next few years, he had a steady costume business and some farming income. In 2011, his business grew exponentially after a teacher contacted him for a custom order. Ren had been selling costumes made by other people in the village, but this custom order made him rethink his business model. He put in manufacturing equipment on-site, in his family's home. Business took off. His combination of premade and custom orders earned him US$1.16 million in 2017. These days he sells all over the world; recent orders have shipped to Vietnam and Korea. International business is expanding because of drop-shipping and AliExpress, a site that bridges foreign buyers with small businesses in China, like Ren's. His nephew even gave up a lucrative software development job in a nearby city to come back and help run the Taobao store.

The local government is more than willing to take credit now for such e-commerce success, but Ren explains that he was a lone agent for a long time. The local government had absolutely no idea what Ren was doing in his workshop. In 2012, the newly elected county party secretary, Su, visited local homes in the area, including Ren's. Su was appalled. The computer was in the kitchen, fabric scraps were piled high, and costumes were draped all over the house. Su was alarmed by the fire hazard. When he asked Ren what was going on, Ren told him that it was e-commerce on Taobao (*dianshang*, 电商).

Ren explained that he and his family made costumes, put them on the computer, and sold them for money. Su was mystified—how do you put costumes *on* a computer? How do you then sell them *online*? After Su stormed off, Ren and his family were nervous that the local government would force them to shut their operation down.

Instead, after making some phone calls and asking higher-ups in bigger towns what Taobao was, Su came back to Ren with a proposition. Su thought that e-commerce could be a path for economic development in the village, and tasked Ren with teaching other villagers how to become e-commerce entrepreneurs.

The fear of getting shut down still lingers. Ren points to a MODEL BUSINESS UNIT plaque in his office. "For a long time, we paid a small fee to the local government for them to leave us alone. That was about it. We received no support from the government but at least they didn't bother us. And one day, I hear a knock on the door. I see that it's the local officials, and I think . . . Oh no. I really didn't want to open the door, because we're peasants, traditionally we don't have great relationships with government . . . we really don't want to get involved with government stuff, we're not educated like government people. I ignore the knocks until someone knocks so hard that I think the door is going to fall off. When I open the door, they present me with this plaque, 'Model Business Unit.'" Ren chuckles.

Ren is now the village party secretary, a government person himself. "I didn't want to be village party secretary. It's exhausting—there's so much work. I still have to run the company as well as raise our kids and attend to village affairs. But the village voted me in. And they voted me in so I will try my best to do the job. My biggest priority is to make the village a better place to live."

Which explains Ren's all-out war on poplar trees. He's convinced that the trees are taking up valuable arable land. With the influx of e-commerce money, the village can afford to plant lucrative cash crops and replace poplar trees with fruit trees. Ren says that the most popular cash crop in the village among the younger generation is chili peppers. Since the chilies require less land to farm, young farmers also make extra income by renting out their land. And while he finds this practice odd, since Shandong's climate is not particularly amenable to chili growing, he doesn't expect the younger generation to have the same attitude toward the environment that he has. He acknowledges that their relationship to farming is different.

When I get back to the United States, I search for Snow White costumes on Amazon. Drop-shippers are plentiful on Amazon these days—the business model has taken over much of Amazon, and American e-commerce. Unlike traditional shops, drop-shippers don't keep anything in stock themselves, but order directly from a third party to have the item sent to a seller. The global reach of drop-shipping is born out of Alibaba and AliExpress, allowing drop-shipping entrepreneurs access to millions of items, shipped at low cost, directly from China. There are numerous online articles about how to start a profitable drop-shipping business, and many of these businesses are responsible for the deluge of Instagram ads that you see: lifestyle brands selling sleek water bottles, new travel bags, and suitcases. These items are often from AliExpress: drop-shippers simply provide the advertising and marketing.

After a few pages of scrolling, I find the costume that Ren makes, distinctive in the gold edging on the front triangle panel, a detail not in the cartoon Snow White's original dress. It's a difficult-to-explain feeling, but it's like having a family member or friend become famous and seeing them in a movie—a disconnect in my personal perception of scale and distance. It feels like I am getting away with something. There's a perversity about it, a brief flash of familiarity in a global economy that requires namelessness. It feels bizarre: a group of children trick-or-treating in suburban America is fueling the growth of fruit trees and chili peppers in Shandong, and also driving land rentals. The internet is tangibly reshaping Dinglou's environment.

7.

There are a few things that clearly do not exist in Dinglou. Among them: Halloween, nature, family boundaries, and hard currency. Halloween is not celebrated in China, except for in some urban pockets of Beijing and Shanghai, and increasingly parents and the government alike are troubled by the Western, Christian connotations of Halloween. In Dinglou, Halloween is not a holiday but a time for extra work spent between the family workshop and harvest.

Nature is just as elusive. For urbanites across the world, nature exists as either a natural resource or a park to be conserved in imagined untamed beauty. Dinglou's nature is ugly and bare. It's a force of its own. Each centimeter of Dinglou's land has been planted or tilled, touched by humans in some way, including the dead. When villagers die, they are buried in the dusty yellow fields, graves marked by small stones, tucked in between plots of vegetables and wheat. While sustainable agriculture was practiced in China for thousands of years, the urbanization and industrialization of the 1980s pressured villagers to require more from their relationship to nature. Being a Taobao village has worsened this, creating added pollution and waste. A once complex relationship to nature has flattened and been diminished to cash cropping, the earth becoming factory, once rich soil becoming dirt.

The lack of family boundaries is what gave rise to Ren's business. He's since repaid his relatives for his initial RMB 1,400 loan. This type of intra-family lending is enormously popular across China, deemed "economic Confucianism" by some. Children are expected to be filial and pay for parental expenses, returning the hard work that parents put into raising them. Distant cousins in rural villages will ask wealthy city relatives for business startup funds. This type of payment and lending has become so common that the 2019 Chinese New Year's Spring Festival Gala (an annual, widely watched TV event) began with a skit on *sifangqian* (私房钱), or one's private money, and the hijinks of a husband and wife both sneakily sending money to family members via mobile payment. And as the government steps away from welfare structures and pensions, the family bank becomes ever more necessary to keep the elderly from sliding into poverty. In 2018, a widely circulated online survey by Toutiao, a popular news app, revealed that 54 percent of parents rely on their children to cover living expenses.

The family is central as an economic unit. And like any economy, the confluence of family and money creates drama. Rites of marriage and birth are emphasized as the way this economic network of family expands—rituals with their own growing pains. But for now, the government is banking on "traditional family values" to keep the family unit together, pushing an image of smiling, idealized heteronormativity across all forms of media.[1]

The lack of hard currency in Dinglou indicates that traditional banks have been replaced. Few transactions in the village involve actual cash—instead, mobile payment is the easiest way to buy sesame oil or wholesale costumes. This is done entirely through Alipay. Alipay has become a financial institution contained in a mobile device. All across China, mobile payment has replaced cash. For sellers like Ren, Alipay has solved the issue of nervously checking bank accounts every day after an order ships.

Alipay functions as a sophisticated escrow account. A buyer can send money to a seller via Alipay and Alipay holds the money. The platform releases the money to the seller once the buyer indicates he or she has received the goods. Sending secret money to your parents while avoiding the ire of your spouse can now be done through Alipay. Loans can also be taken out through Alipay, which is popular among younger generations and bemoaned as the downfall of Chinese society by older generations. Alipay has become a pivotal part of rural economic infrastructure, in areas where traditional physical banking has been inconvenient for many villagers like Ren Qingsheng.

In 2019, Alipay had seven hundred million users, with nearly two hundred million transactions a day. It also has a credit-scoring system, Sesame Credit, for Alipay loans, which is often confused with a national-credit scoring system. But most important of all, Alipay solved the problem of trust between buyers and sellers—a critical issue in "platform businesses" and a management idea that originated in Japan in the 1990s, from business gurus such as Jiro Kokuryo and Imai Kenichi.

Alipay has even more ambitious plans. At Ant Financial, Alibaba's sister firm that now owns Alipay, entire branches of the company are devoted to rural finance. At one talk I attended in Guangzhou, Zheng Jia, the deputy general manager of Ant Financial's rural finance department, pointed to an elaborate diagram showing how Alipay will plug into rural economies. Alibaba's ET Agricultural Brain will help farmers generate greater income. Increased income will facilitate the purchasing of more farming equipment, off Alibaba's many other e-commerce platforms. Jia showed an elaborate computer vision project that is already being piloted in Henan Province. Farmers need access to loans, Jia said. But they typically have types of collateral that are different from those of city people. A farmer's assets might be pigs or chickens. As a result, Ant Financial is setting up cameras on farms that can display a farmer's assets in real time to help assess credit scores and risk in lending scenarios. Such data can also be used by ET Agricultural Brain to help farmers with the animal-raising process. With this risk-assessment camera in place, farmers can then use Alipay to apply for loans. Already, a chicken farmer in Lankao County, Henan, has used this complex Bio-Inventory of Assets System to apply for RMB 200,000 in loans on Alipay.

Will these platforms continue to run unfettered and unregulated? A lawyer I talk to, who has worked at places like the China Food and Drug Administration, points to very public, visible platform safety incidents that indicate regulation will happen. He gives examples: people getting sick from food purchased off Taobao, rural citizens getting scammed into bankruptcy by peer-to-peer lending platforms, and the Didi Chuxing incident in 2018, where a driver raped and killed a passenger. The public outcry in response to these incidents led swiftly to immediate changes to the platform. The government is happy to intervene, even in an age where it has been more and more open to letting private companies act first, and regulating only later.

8.

In 2001, after the September 11 terrorist attacks, President George W. Bush took to television to deliver an important message: Above all, stay calm, go on with your daily life, and keep shopping. Fifteen years later, after the election of President Trump, some activists on the left had a similar message: Vote with your wallet. There was not much you could do about the administration in power, but what you could do was abstain from buying certain brands.

Shopping has made consumption the site of political action rather than the enemy of it. Although many of us have jobs that keep us occupied, the real work we do these days is shopping, and especially shopping online. Economists across the world make it clear that we are in a consumer-driven economy. Shopping is an ecstasy-inducing act, a brief tease that allows us to brush up against the life we desire, that we feel like we deserve. So much exists in the service of shopping, one of the world's biggest religions. Modern corporate social media is born out of shopping—it fills our screens, bits of news and personal announcements interspersed with ads, enrapturing us into a ludic loop. Machine-learning algorithms hum along to recommend better items. Entire companies like Facebook and Tencent derive vast profits from ads, collecting and monetizing data to sell better ads. Smaller platforms scheme on how to collect data to resell for marketers.

There is no end to shopping, for Dinglou or for us in the United States. Dinglou was China's first Taobao village, but thousands more like it exist, making everything from wooden toys to clothing, candy, and computer fans. These items end up not only in China but abroad. While there are casualties of the trade war between the United States and China, with titans of globalization such as Walmart under threat, these smaller e-commerce manufacturing businesses in China are thriving in the long tail of shopping.

Sellers on Amazon, independent drop-shippers, and platforms like Wish.com use the power of AliExpress to tap into these small manufacturers throughout China, in places like Dinglou. Curated Instagram campaigns, featuring prominent influencers, are launched by a vast landscape of small, new "lifestyle brands"—companies based outside China that source directly from AliExpress. Manufacturers on AliExpress also move with lightning speed in customizing designs. Many crowdfunded products made on Kickstarter are produced by these small manufacturers as well. Wish.com, with headquarters based in Menlo Park, is a peculiar version of Amazon with half a billion users. It is a drop-shipper, sourcing from AliExpress, but its customer base is in the Midwest, Texas, and Florida. Its diverse users range from those who frequent flea markets and swap meets to racists who post on 4chan about the "cheap chink gear" available.

One of my favorite newsletters, *The Strategist* (a weekly dispatch of shopping deals from *New York* magazine), recommends that I buy the very hyped Orolay down coat, a "viral" coat exclusively available on Amazon.com with more than seven thousand reviews. Priced at US$130, and with a four-star rating, it seems like a good deal. Man

Repeller, a well-known fashion blog, agrees, saying the coat has "murky origins" but that it recommends the 90 percent down jacket. The murky origin, it turns out, is rural China. Jiaxing county, Zhejiang to be precise, where locals work for Orolay, churning out these down jackets and taking advantage of Amazon's new measures that make it easy for overseas businesses to sell on the site.

Matilda, the founder of Bits x Bites, had put it this way: If big companies like Nabisco symbolized the nineties, hundreds of smaller, fragmented companies will dominate the future, catering to a continuum of different tastes and experiences. And this landscape of smaller companies is what some people see as part of "the New Retail." This New Retail will be powered by the edges of manufacturing, in places like Dinglou.

Shopping is powerful. It can swiftly accommodate broad cultural shifts, responding to the myriad subcultures and identities in the internet age. A scan through Taobao, Etsy, Instagram, and Xiaohongshu (the Chinese version of Instagram) shows enticing products in ads that fit almost any identity that you can think of.

Ads mesmerize us by instilling a "cruel optimism," a relation that the theorist Lauren Berlant describes as when "the object that you thought would bring happiness becomes an object that deteriorates the conditions for happiness. But its presence represents the possibility of happiness as such."[2] An example she gives is the dream of "the good life," where the good life eludes most of us, given the current economic reality we live in, as many of us live paycheck to paycheck. Yet we chase after this dream, some of us styling ourselves and our homes to reflect the life we aspire to, while plunging ourselves into debt, losing relationships to overworking. This isn't just in the United States—it's in China too, where millennials have nearly doubled the country's household debt through aspirational spending.[3]

Unlike religion though, shopping traverses your innermost wishes, requiring your faith and desire, only to leave you stranded without community or security. Luckily, there is always a beautiful ad around the corner, waiting for you, to ignite that faith, that longing and attachment.

Taobao is technically a free platform, but it makes money from sellers buying ads. When I spoke to Ren, he pragmatically likened it to a form of digital rent: it's more expensive to run a store in a busy part of town with better foot traffic.

A few blocks down from Ren's house, I stop at a shoe shop. It's unavoidable—there's an alarmingly strong scent of plastic emanating from the doorway. The owner of this shoe store disagrees with Ren. Not only has the drive for ads gotten worse, but Taobao launched seller livestreaming, a version of an online home-shopping network. This takes additional time and resources from sellers. These ads are different from a form of rent—livestream requires that the seller offer something beyond the product itself, something akin to aura or alluring aspiration. Standing in the shop, I'm dizzy from the fumes, tired of Dinglou's aura. The owner seems to be tired as well.

"Alibaba sucks us dry," he says. "It sucks the blood out of us, and it will suck the blood out of this village. As sellers, all our money is kept in Alipay because that's how buyers send money. At the drop of a pin they can demand a refund, and because of the escrow service, the money gets sent back to them, even if I've shipped the order already. Or maybe they don't like the material, they think it's cheap. But we have to keep on making worse-quality stuff. How are we supposed to keep prices low and also compete with others? The government thinks it's great and keeps doing things like building roads, putting in broadband. And Alibaba uses all this infrastructure for free, relies on us to make decisions on lowering the quality of goods. But what happens next? There's only so much cutting corners we can do. There's only so many ads we can buy, lies about the products we can say. What happens when this system fails?"

9.

As the sun sets in Dinglou, people begin to set up stalls for the night market, rolling out metal carts and tiny stools. This night market happens every ninth day, according to the traditional lunar Chinese calendar that is widely used in rural China, as opposed to the urban Gregorian calendar. This lunar calendar is based on agricultural planting seasons, carving time into unequal, inconsistent slivers.

Like any cult, shopping is difficult to extricate oneself from. I love shopping. I am unashamed. Even when I'm away from home, staying in Dinglou, I know that packages might be piling up at my door. I buy wrapping paper from Amazon, envelopes, rolls of tape, the perfect summer cooler for storing seltzer, a set of spice jars. They are all generic items by brands I've never heard of, items that can be easily found on Alibaba or AliExpress. I know I pay a slight premium by purchasing via the sellers on Amazon who source from Alibaba. Sometimes I buy handmade goods from Etsy, lovely items but still made out of fabric manufactured in southern China.

Online shopping is a meditative act for me, as I read reviews, peruse blogs, and contemplate the potential of my life with this new product. I page through Xiaohongshu and Instagram; I savor ads for their aesthetics as much as their aspiration. There are two consumerist logics prevalent in my circle of left-leaning urbanites. Political action in shopping is positioned as either refusing to purchase or purchasing from brands that you support. It's a parallel I see in approaches to managing relations to social media: either log off entirely or switch to a different network. And while it's easy to acknowledge that I don't need a Snow White costume, it's harder to say I wouldn't be slightly happier with a modernist glass carafe or a plastic-free bamboo toothbrush. At least, happier for a few moments.

Refusal and purchasing to support are both cruel optimism, providing a false sense of control. It's that same sense of control that makes shopping so pleasurable. In a world that is so interconnected, with problems at a scale I cannot comprehend—climate change, plastics in the ocean, e-waste, political instability from globalization—the trick of shopping is that it makes me feel like I am doing something about those problems. I am asserting my agency, this agency that I am promised as an American. My small choice to either buy or not buy exerts control over the world as I want to see it—as I imagine it, maybe more eco-friendly, more sustainable.

But what if I didn't need to assert control at all? What would it mean to define my daily life without any of the packages that arrive at my doorstep, to invent a life that required no material possessions? And while the thought of giving up control sounds nice, in the meantime, I scroll, click, read, add to cart. Somewhere, not in Dinglou but likely in another village in China, a nice family is making me a wooden toothbrush with removable heads that will arrive at my door on a subscription basis. It's eco-friendly.

In 2018, Alibaba announced plans to export the Taobao village model. The World Bank is interested in this model for other places in the world, including countries like South Africa. One former counsel for Alibaba tells me that Jack Ma envisioned the Electronic World Trade Organization (eWTO), before counsel advised him to change the name. It's now called the Electronic World Trade Platform, or eWTP. The eWTP has become part of China's Belt and Road Initiative. As of 2018, three eWTP outposts had been set up: in Malaysia, Rwanda, and South Africa. The Alibaba Research Institute's rural researchers continue to monitor manufacturing costs throughout the Chinese countryside as well as in the United States, citing the extensive investment Chinese companies are now undertaking in revitalizing rural American towns.

Before I left his shop, the disgruntled shoe manufacturer kept saying, "It's all a scam." His words had the solemnity of a mantra.

How to Eat the World

"Software is eating the world," declared Marc Andreessen in 2011, and in a sense, he was right. In a time of crisis, software has increasingly become the answer to help us build and support more efficient systems. The software industry has also been responsible for enormous inequality by accelerating other industries like rare earth mining and gig work. While software may be eating the world, this is *not* inevitable. The promise of software and technology is that they help solve the problems we face right now, without addressing how those problems began—problems including the uneven distribution of basic resources like food. This recipe imagines a world where we have continued using technology simply to solve problems, without taking time to think about the maintenance and care of what we have in front of us.

Ingredients for Wrappers

glutinous rice flour | 45 g

rice flour (water-milled, Thai variety) | 45 g

wheat starch | 20 g

powdered sugar | 30 g

coconut milk | 130 ml

vegetable oil | 18 g
glutinous rice flour for covering surfaces and kneading

Ingredients for Filling

butter | 45 g
moon-maize meal | 40 g, may substitute for regular cornmeal
powdered cream | 40 g, may substitute with powdered milk
powdered sugar | 30 g, may add 5 g more for a sweeter filling
eggs | 2 large

Tools

heat-proof spatula
steamer
metal dish or bowl that fits inside the steamer
large metal bowl | for making the filling
mold | for shaping the mooncakes; this can be as simple as a muffin tin, or, if you wish, you may purchase a more complex decorative mold online

These delicate "ice skin" mooncakes have wrappers made of glutinous rice flour instead of the traditional wheat flour, making it a delicious, southern-style Chinese treat. They are a favorite for the mid-autumn festival.

The filling of these mooncakes is a moon-maize custard, a custard with depth that complements the traditional glutinous rice wrappers perfectly. In 2018, the first experiments by the China Lunar Exploration Program's Chang'e 4 moon lander established a self-contained ecosystem for agriculture on the moon. It was the first time any biological matter grew on the moon.[4] The next missions, Chang'e 5 and 6, advanced moon agriculture. Moon-maize seed cultivars were quickly developed by the company Syngenta, and were specially engineered to withstand lowered gravitational fields and less water.

While moon living hasn't taken off as predicted in the past few years, the popularity of moon-grown foods has soared. As fires, pollution, and climate change worsened, farming on earth produced increasingly low-quality, low-nutrition foods, including some vegetables tainted with cadmium or lead. Automated farming on the moon took off, in response to upper-middle-class consumer demand. For those who can afford it, moon-cultivated foods are not only higher in nutrients but also far healthier. Studies have shown that the average lifespan of someone eating earth-cultivated foods is about fifty years, while those eating moon-cultivated food since birth can live up to a hundred years on average.

Gourmands also insist that the moon's terroir, the special moon-maize cultivar, coupled with the unique gravitational field of the moon, give a complex, hearty aroma to moon-farmed foods. Moon maize is not just a specialty crop, however. Currently, private farming companies are doing research in using small, cost-effective UAVs (unmanned autonomous vehicles) for sowing and harvesting, so that everyone on earth can access moon-farmed food.

For this recipe, we highly suggest using the "Lora" strain, as it is organically grown and combines the best of heritage maize with the sweetness of modern corn. While these moon-maize mooncakes fetch a hefty price at Hema, you can make them at home for a fraction of the cost.

Take care to cover the finished mooncakes well, to prevent them from drying out. Happy Chang'e Festival![5]

To Make the Wrappers

Combine the glutinous rice flour, rice flour, wheat starch, powdered sugar, coconut milk, and vegetable oil in a bowl. Whisk together until smooth—it's important to make sure there are no lumps. The wrapper mix should now be a thick texture, similar to glue.

Put the wrapper mixture in a deep metal bowl or plate, the one that fits inside your steamer. Steam on high for 15 minutes.

Remove the metal bowl from the steamer. Take the dough out carefully since it's hot. Place onto a kneading surface that is lightly dusted with glutinous rice flour.

Knead the dough vigorously for 5 to 10 minutes, incorporating more glutinous rice flour so it does not stick to the kneading surface. The dough will start to feel smoother and oilier as you knead.

Cover the dough tightly in plastic wrap and put it in the fridge. Keep refrigerated for 2 hours.

To Make the Filling

In a large metal bowl, combine butter (sliced into pieces), moon-maize meal, powdered cream, and powdered sugar. Place the metal bowl over a pot that has boiling water in it, so that the metal bowl functions as a double boiler—this way the custard will not stick to the bowl. Stir until butter is melted and contents are well mixed. Add the two eggs and whisk until the mixture is smooth. Keep whisking until the mixture starts to thicken into a paste. The custard is done once the paste no longer sticks to the sides of the bowl or the spatula.

Transfer the filling into a smaller container and cover with plastic wrap. Refrigerate the filling for 2 hours.

Assemble the Mooncakes

After the wrapper and filling have cooled, put glutinous rice flour on a surface to assemble the mooncakes. Measure the wrappers into 20–25 g balls, depending on the size of your mold. Measure the filling into 25–30 g balls. Using a rolling pin, flatten the wrapper balls. Dust one side of each wrapper with rice flour so that it does not stick to the mold. If using a wooden mold, put the wrapper on top of the mold. Place filling inside the wrapper. Wrap ends and gently press (make sure not to press too forcefully, otherwise the filling might break through). Remove from mold. Dust the mooncakes with rice flour before storing so that they do not stick to each other.

.8.

Welcome to My Pearl Party

1.

My hand is deep inside a large mussel, fingers searching for small round pearls through light pink flesh. "Yeah, we feed these mussels chicken and pig poop, so you might want to wash your hands after this," says my host, Zhao. Inside a large shell about twenty centimeters tall and ten centimeters wide is a mass of pearls stuck to the interior. One by one, through the film of slimy water on mussel meat, I remove each of these pearls and put them in a red plastic bucket.

It's a gray, cloudy day, and I am standing next to pearl mussel ponds, with the fuzzy outline of mountains in the background. There's a little hut nearby, for shelter. It's built with torn tin, some wood, and plastic sheeting. A barking, mangy dog whose sole purpose is to protect these ponds from pearl thieves is chained next to it. Narrow, unpaved muddy roads form a grid across these ponds. There are some other people on small metal boats, tending to mussels. Zhao is dressed in a jean jacket, shivering in the cold, with fresh white sneakers that have somehow managed to stay clean despite the mud.

Over 70 percent of the world's freshwater pearls come

from China, and the vast majority come from ponds like the ones I am visiting, in a rural area near the city of Zhuji, in Zhejiang Province. Zhuji has been nicknamed "the Pearl City" because of its pearl production. I'm about an hour outside Zhuji, at a production site in Shanxiahu Village. Zhao, a vivacious man in his late twenties, has the demeanor of a Silicon Valley CEO. It's the only way I can describe it—his mannerisms, his long, carefully phrased speeches that burst with excitement, his proclamations about how he is disrupting the pearl industry, and his inability to let any part of the conversation fall silent. He's talking, telling me about his vision, asking his director of marketing to show me an image, trying to convince me of their future plans. His hair is choppily cut, and he's constantly gesturing, pointing, making strange shapes using his hands that suggest boxes, clean slates, or explosions. *New. Outside of the box. Different.*

Zhao and his company's director of marketing, Lisa, had come to pick me up from the Zhuji train station. He immediately took us out to eat. We sit in a small restaurant that has discarded napkins all over the floor. The local specialty is a bowl of noodles with tiny shrimps that have grown alarmingly large claws. Another, much more delicious, local treat is mochi-like dumplings made with sticky rice wrappers, filled with finely minced vegetables. "What we're doing here," he says, "we're changing the pearl industry. We're shaking things up. Those old heads you see at the pearl market, they don't know what's coming to them." He slurps a noodle loudly and tosses an empty shrimp shell on the table.

Zhao runs a small, agile pearl company with his wife

and two friends, all of them under the age of thirty. If he's the firecracker CEO who swaggers around with a mission, his friend who takes us out onto the mussel ponds plays the restrained, tireless CTO (chief technical officer) trope. Unlike the other pearl companies, which rely on a vast network of employees and facilities, Zhao's company runs lean. They have only a few pearl ponds, emphasizing quality of pearls over quantity. Instead of hiring their own employees, they siphon off the services of mussel opening and pearl sorting from other pearl companies.

Agile methods have been at the heart of modern technology's growth. While hardware advances have enabled more sophisticated software, such software would not exist without the particular working processes and collaboration methods that bind tech companies together. These processes that enable companies to run lean draw upon *gemba kaizen*, or the art of continuous improvement, pioneered by Japanese management consultants. *Gemba kaizen* emphasizes cutting away waste, and ensuring that workers and managers are aligned, decreasing miscommunications and wasted time, known as "thrash." Originally used as a working process in Japanese manufacturing, agile methods in software are now spilling back over into other industries. Zhao's company is small and agile—continuously evaluating and reevaluating future plans and past mistakes, making sure communication is clear, always syncing managers and workers up with one another.

"Raising pearl oysters is not easy," his CTO tells me, as he stands in rain boots, camouflage-patterned pants, and a black jacket with muddy paw prints on it. He gestures to the ponds. Each of these ponds features floating soda bottles. We're currently standing next to what I jokingly call the Sprite-sponsored pond. The bottles bob on top of the pond like lane markers in a swimming pool. Beneath each of the bottles is a webbed net that contains several large pearl mussels.

"It takes five years to get a good pearl, and you have to seed these mussels, with flesh from another mussel. Each of the pearls starts off as a round piece of flesh from another mussel. Another thing is maintenance. The mussels are bottom-feeders, and we feed them chicken and pig feces. But if you put too much in, algal blooms start to form and choke up the mussels. Algae loves warm water, which does make pearls grow faster. One of the hardest parts is raising the next cycle of mussels, since when they reproduce, the larvae stick to fish gills. You have to really use a lot of water to force the larvae to come off the fish and to grow into a large-enough mussel."

Zhao's father-in-law was one of the earliest pearl farmers in the Shanxiahu area and a pioneer of the industry. While pearl farming has existed in China since the thirteenth century, it wasn't until the 1980s that it became industrialized under China's "reform and opening up," initiated by Deng Xiaoping, when the state enacted policies for market privatization. The change in production scale demanded a shift in mussel species as well. Early industrial-scale farmers like Zhao's father-in-law started switching to the *Hyriopsis cumingi* mussel, the "three-corner mussel" (*sanjiaobang*, 三角蚌), which has far higher pearl yields than traditional mussels. The local ecology has changed drastically since the 1980s, with waterways becoming inundated with excess nitrogen and phosphorus from the animal feces that feed the mussels.

Located in the south of China, with the Yangtze River running through it, Zhejiang is blessed with an abundance of water from plentiful ponds, groundwater, and favorable rains. In fact, the "glut" of water in the south has existed for thousands of years, with Xi Jinping recently trying to revive an ancient plan to funnel water from the south to the dry north. While Zhao's father-in-law originally used public ponds for his mussels, the government started to regulate the industrial uses of public waterways in the 1990s. Farmers scrambled to turn their tiny plots of land into lucrative pearl ponds instead. In 2017, the town of Shanxiahu and the surrounding villages produced a thousand tons of pearls, making the area the global epicenter of cultured pearls.

2.

"I mean, the thing is, I came back because I knew that it's easy to do business when all the existing companies you know are run by stupid people, by simpletons," Zhao proclaims loudly. We're in his office, which is located on the first floor of his three-story home, overlooking a canal and bridge. It's peaceful. His office is all white, with track lighting and shoddy replicas of mid-century modern furniture. There's a receipt printer that is constantly spewing out new orders, and a jewelry-making station that his wife sits at, with hand-knit gray fingerless gloves on. It's chilly inside, so we're all still wearing our coats.

Southern China is notorious for not having central

heating. It was an arbitrary city-planning decision made back in the 1950s, for northern China to have central heating provided by the government, but southern China to be left to its own devices.[1] The government recently decided to crack down on air pollution in an attempt to build an "ecological civilization," so cheap coal heating is being replaced with natural gas or electric heaters. Wages remain low in the countryside, and household heating is a luxury.[2] Zhao's office is especially cold today, after yesterday's snowfall.

Across the canal, Zhao's childhood friend happens to be getting married. It's an auspicious day, Zhao jokes, with a wedding and a visit from an American. Large golden elephants and an inflatable red awning greet visitors to the village. A brass marching band is playing, and fresh flowers line the streets. The village economy has been buoyed by the pearl business, and wealth seems to be everywhere.

Zhao has a bachelor's degree in economics, from a small college in the city of Hangzhou. Life at school was carefree, if boring at a certain point, which led Zhao to finding some creative ways to fill time.

"I mean, I've done it all. I even had a side job as a food delivery courier. Which is weird, right? Most of the kids I grew up with, they either never went to college or their parents struck it rich in the pearl business and sent them to college with loads of money. They were *fuerdai* [富二代, a commonly used term for well-off, rich kids]. But man, I couldn't just sit there and do nothing like these *fuerdai*. My parents didn't have money. I worked so hard to get to college. I'm not stupid. But I just knew I couldn't win in the city, not against kids whose parents do have money."

I ask Zhao what his dad did for work. "Manual labor. He sold his labor. Do you know how difficult that kind of work is? These houses in this village, these beautiful houses, he built most of them. He's only sixty now, but man, he worked so hard he can barely walk now. Has back problems."

Hustling and fate brought Zhao back to his hometown. He tells me he was sick of city life. Besides, he says, after he got married he and his wife had a son; their son has autism.

"I'm the kind of person who's liable to drift off . . . which I did in the city, during college. I did KTV [karaoke], hung out in bars, all that low-life stuff. But I saw my future before me, I knew I could never afford a house in the city and my kid's school fees. This is what happens when you come from nothing. I knew I needed to build something and I needed a quiet place to do it. To be part of *shehui* [社会, society], to *hun shehui* [混社会, get by in society], you need to have a strategy," Zhao says philosophically.

Zhao's business now has clients from all over the world—Italians, Japanese, British. He points out repeatedly that he specializes in the best pearls only, because he was sick and tired of "the trash that comes out of Zhuji, that gives us all a bad name." "What I'm trying to do," he says, "is to build a market, an ecosystem, by creating a company that runs lean, producing consistent, quality pearls. For so long, in Zhuji, we've been known for making low-quality pearls, or even fakes. Instead, I'll pick maybe one hundred pearls out of a harvest of one thousand to sell to clients. The rest of them, those nine hundred low-quality pearls, I'll sell back to people at the market in Zhuji. They'll buy them and resell them. Or, if it's too low quality, I'll make it into pearl powder."

Not missing a beat, he peers at me. "I mean, you could use some pearl powder. It's good for your skin, it unclogs pores and whitens you up. You could really, really use some pearl powder."

3.

Zhuji is proud of its status as a pearl city, and it even includes the Angel's Tears Pearl Museum. Like Shenzhen's Huaqiangbei for electronics, Zhuji's pearl market is a dizzying array of stalls and booths. The pearl market is filled with the loud noises of yelling and bargaining, bright fluorescent lights, and pearls everywhere. Handbags made of pearls, pearl necklaces, pearls by the ton.

A global crowd frequents this market, buying pearls in bulk and then reselling them back in their respective countries. Indians, Japanese, Nigerians, Europeans, all roam the market, looking for the best deals. Calculators displaying numbers (the offering amount) are passed back and forth until someone finally relents.

"I hate this market," says Zhao. "This is no way to do business," and I agree, sweaty and getting what I call "the market flu."

The market flu can strike at any time, but it often does under the overwhelming, bright fluorescent lights of a wholesale market. It's a kind of jitteriness where you can't pay attention to a single thing, where you're distracted by shiny objects everywhere. You leave the market feeling a buzz, uncertain how much time passed between when you first entered and when you left. In places like Shanxiahu, Yiwu, or Huaqiangbei, in Shenzhen, what I experience as the market flu, others experience as the smell of money and hustle.

Anywhere there is money to be made, fakes proliferate, and cons happen. Some sellers at the market offer the lowest-quality pearls, seeded with plastic instead of mussel flesh. Only the thinnest layer of lacquer forms on the plastic, yielding large pearls in a short amount of time. This budget method is unlike tissue nucleation, where a mussel deposits lacquer for up to five years.

Other types of fakery include changing the color of a pearl, which allows sellers to convince buyers that it is a different type of pearl, like a sea pearl. Mabe-type pearls are also easily faked, by sanding cheaper pearls sawed in half.

The ultimate scam that Shanxiahu sellers pull is so brash that I am not sure I would call it a scam. Zhao points out to me two people standing over a bin with calipers, examining a pearl necklace. "The calipers say it's 6.5 millimeters, right?" he asks. I nod.

"Well, here at Shanxiahu pearl market, a 6.5 is a 7.00!" He laughs, cackling at how Shanxiahu sellers intentionally misread a caliper's measurements to exaggerate a pearl's size.

In a somber tone, he says, "The thing that makes these older, traditional sellers extra stupid is that they don't realize fakes give our market a bad name. It's an ecosystem. The last thing I want our village, our market, or even our country to be known for is fake pearls. It drives the price of good pearls down, and makes people feel like they can ask us for lower and lower prices."

The longer I spend with Zhao and his team, the more I learn about the different kinds of pearls. Baroque pearls, akoya pearls, Edison pearls, sea pearls, abalone pearls, cassis pearls, oblong pearls that look like puffed rice, pearls so perfectly round that you would swear they were made in a laboratory. And of course, wish pearls. Wish pearls are the reason I came here in the first place. Wish pearl oysters are small, dead oysters that have a pearl inside. These oysters are vacuum sealed and shipped all the way to places in the United States. Zhao doesn't sell any wish pearl oysters, but he knows of a few companies that do, in case I want some.

Perusing Alibaba.com, I see that most wish pearl manufacturers are located in Zhuji. In order to get these wish pearl oysters into the United States, Zhao tells me, I need a wildlife permit, even though the oysters are already dead.

4.

It's a Friday night in early 2017 and I'm sitting at home in California, leisurely watching Facebook Live. After a tumultuous political news cycle, I've found relaxation in crevices of the internet like livestream. There are ten thousand other people also watching Kristie's Krazy Kultured Pearl Parties livestream. Kristie herself is on-screen, singing: "Like a pearl-gin! Shuckin' for the very first time!" to the tune of Madonna's "Like a Virgin." Kristie is a thirty-six-year-old white woman from Georgia who has a Facebook pearl empire. Her page, Kristie's Krazy Kultured Pearl Parties, has over fifty thousand likes.

She sticks her hand into a plastic jar, riffles around,

and pulls out a small oyster. "Jessica's first oyster! What will it beeeeeeeee?" Kristie shrieks, with great suspense. "Will it be twins?"

What I'm watching this evening is a pearl party—it's like a Tupperware party for the Facebook age, where hostesses sell goods on social media livestream. Selling parties like this are not just for pearls. These days, the multilevel marketing (MLM) industry is thriving on social media as millions of people hawk aromatherapy oils, yoga leggings, and vitamins across Instagram and Facebook. While MLMs have been known for their predatory, pyramid-scheme structures, some MLMs, like Rodan + Fields, are now legitimizing themselves, sporting luxe offices in downtown San Francisco, near Salesforce and Google. Other companies, like the venture-capital-funded Stella & Dot, proliferate throughout my own Facebook feed, relentless in their quest to have me join the craze as a seller.

The pearls Kristie sells are low quality, but the oyster Kristie has in her hand is special to me. It's a wish pearl oyster, the same dead mollusk that Zhao told me about, flown halfway around the world, trucked through a series of warehouses all the way from Shanxiahu.

As a pearl party participant, you can watch on Facebook Live, and you can also reserve an oyster by filling in an order form before the scheduled party. Reserving the oyster is around US$20, and you keep whatever pearl is inside the oyster. You get to watch as the oyster is opened for you on Facebook Live during the broadcast by the hostess. She typically calls herself a "pearl consultant" for a multilevel marketing company that distributes these oysters. As a consultant, she purchases the wish pearl oysters from the MLM company up front, and there's pressure for her to sell as many as she can, otherwise she's stuck with oysters that she's unable to off-load. All oysters have a pearl in them, and sometimes two, which is known in pearl party parlance as "getting twins." After opening the oyster and cleaning the pearl, the hostess sends the pearl back to the MLM company, which prepares the pearl in your choice of jewelry setting—a dog-shaped key chain, or a silver-plated oyster necklace, conveniently shipped to you.

Kristie is an independent Vantel Pearls consultant. Vantel, like most MLM companies, requires you to pay up front for any goods you want to sell. Whether you manage to sell what you've purchased is your responsibility as an entrepreneur. Add-ons like business tips and strategies can also be purchased, and part of your own operating costs includes buying lots of ads, on Facebook and other social media.

Over the past year, Kristie has been gathering up acolytes: "direct downlines" that report to her and host their own pearl parties. Other pearl party hostesses have their own empires, complete with their own direct downlines.

Kristie's new direct downlines pay an initial flat fee to join her "Pearlfect pearl family," a term she's coined. There's a long Facebook feed with all their introduction videos. Many of them hold pearl parties at times I find surprising—Wednesday at 1:00 p.m., Thursday mornings. Nearly all of the pearl party hostesses are women with southern or midwestern accents, beautifully curved drawls I start to find very soothing.

Direct downlines are a range of people: stay-at-home moms, personal accountants supplementing their income, certified nurse practitioners, or just people who see this pearly life as a way out of their current job. One direct downline is a recently divorced army veteran, trying to find a way to stay at home with her kids. Another direct downline for Kristie used to be a certified nurse practitioner but had to quit because of health issues. She's young, at most thirty, and lives in a tiny town in the Midwest. While most of the hostesses are maniacally cheerful, she has a deep sadness on camera that turns her pearl party into an unintentionally tragic confessional. Her brown eyes are big and dark, her hair dyed purple. Her speech is very gentle and slow. "I didn't feel good yesterday," she says, looking into the camera, "but I thought I'd introduce myself anyways. I used to be a certified nursing assistant. And I had to stop because of back pain on the job. So now I am trying pearl parties. Thanks for watching."

Over 70 percent of MLMers (also known as "direct sellers" in official parlance) are women. The Direct Selling Association proudly notes that "direct selling has an outstanding involvement rate with women and minority groups," and "65% of the survey respondents say that 'flexibility and work-life balance' is a motivation for them." In their introductions on Kristie's Facebook page, the direct downlines all express a desire for more flexibility in taking care of their kids while making money. The three states with the highest percentage of direct sellers are North Dakota, Iowa, and Wyoming. You might be able to guess the next few based on voting data from the 2016 election.

By 2017, almost nineteen million Americans were

engaged in direct selling. North Dakota has the most direct sellers as a percentage of the population and the highest unemployment ranking in the United States. Other states like Iowa, Wyoming, and Montana sit firmly in the overlap between high unemployment and number of direct sellers. Places like Minnesota, Montana, and Georgia all rank in the top ten states with the greatest decline in household income after the 2008 recession. Direct selling is not the cheerful respite from life it appears to be in ads, but a kind of desperate grab at survival.

What Kristie and many others are offering has nothing to do with the product being sold. As I watch more of her videos, I am entranced by the level of thoughtfulness she puts into each oyster opening and the kindness of the community. Comments from viewers flash on the right side of the stream, people sharing stories from their everyday life, cracking jokes with each other. Kristie responds, sometimes with a "God bless" or "You'll be in my prayers." The routine of these videos verges on boring, and in that boredom emerges a repetitive structure. Over the course of a few weeks, the repetitive structure becomes an especially soothing balm for me after hectic days at work.

At a pearl party, the hostess announces your name to the livestream audience, noting where you are from and details about you. As you watch, you can leave comments for the hostess, joining in the conversation, hearing her reply to you in real time. This form of care and attention is moving. As a viewer, you pay for emotional labor. Hostesses make the person whose oyster is about to be opened feel so, so special. And in a time when you rarely get to feel special, doesn't it feel so good to hear that *someone* cares about you?

The model of multilevel marketing, with its emphasis on personal relationships and cultivating entrepreneurship, is not new. It's been around since the 1950s, with Avon makeup and Tupperware. But MLMs really began to gain traction in the 1970s, under a branch of New Age thought called the human potential movement. MLMs thrived in this movement's combination of spiritualism and self-improvement tied to personal wealth attainment. People like the minister and author Norman Vincent Peale sold the power of positive thinking and a "gospel" of prosperity, while entrepreneurs like William Penn Patrick pioneered the MLM tactic of charging sellers in his multilevel marketing company, Holiday Magic, for courses on "mind dynamics." This blend of mysticism and capitalism paved the way for the 1980s, when multilevel marketing morphed into its current form, becoming predatory and insidiously corporate. This form is far more exploitative, wooing people with the illusion of flexible hours and "being your own boss," only to push them deep into debt by getting them to purchase up front thousands of dollars' worth of often unsellable, low-quality merchandise.

During the first dot-com boom of the 1990s, MLM participation soared in response to rising economic inequality. The 1997 book *False Profits: Seeking Financial and Spiritual Deliverance in Multi-Level Marketing and Pyramid Schemes* by Robert Fitzpatrick and Joyce Reynolds documents this first wave of large, corporate MLMs. Despite their predatory nature, these MLMs were further strengthened by the same fiscal deregulation that led to the 2008 recession. Consumers became less shielded by the Federal Trade Commission against MLM practices.

Fitzpatrick and Reynolds saw the rise of MLMs as a response to contemporary social conditions, satisfying the spiritual and socioeconomic needs of a broad swath of Americans. With the American Dream failing, typical social support structures and communities buckled under unregulated capitalism. More people are lured into MLM schemes, becoming sellers. They do so under companies' false promises that they can attain the American Dream. Despite widespread evidence that it's a scam, sellers and buyers alike become seduced by the community and personal connections they experience.

At the end of their book, Fitzpatrick and Reynolds give a portentous warning: Without economic regulation from the government, people would struggle further to attain middle-class stability. Spirituality and community would decrease in their daily lives, under the hustle of materialism. If the government did not try to make the American Dream possible, try to revive community and some kind of shared purpose, citizens would seek another form to manifest their frustrations, becoming enticed into something far worse than MLMs.

The proliferation of MLMs can be easily blamed on social media and technology, just like the spread of misinformation, bizarre health advice, or selfie culture. Yet the reality is more complicated. Social media and online community certainly play a part in accelerating information, as well as in decreasing the barrier of accessing content. But these online interactions are a manifestation of broader socioeconomic conditions. With one of the worst, most error-prone health-care systems in the developed world, why wouldn't you seek out online health advice or alternative explanations for illness in the United States? With deepening job insecurity and the elusiveness of the American Dream, why wouldn't you at least try joining an MLM to sell online?

In that light, the post-2016-election pleas for all of us to log off and just talk to each other in real life are naive. We haven't been talking to one another in real life for a long time. Unless, apparently, we're trying to sell each other something.

In a 2017 interview with *The Atlantic*, Robert Fitzpatrick says MLMs are stronger than ever. The number of people signing up to become direct sellers is increasing. MLMs continue to scam people because "it's a beautiful story, a self-indulgent story, a miraculous story—that in 2017, with all its job insecurity, there is, in America, an alternative, and that alternative is not run by Wall Street or the government. It's a kind of mass hoax. It's a psychological sale first, then an economical sale, and the two work together."

In all of Kristie's videos, she exudes a ridiculous, oblivious privilege as she discusses current events, an uneasy performance of whiteness encoded into her banter. Her audience is mainly white women, turning pearl parties into a kind of mirrored stage play. As I click through her followers and their posts, I find a repetitive conspiratorial tone. Some are clearly evangelical Christians, and others post videos about the deep state. In a time of precariousness, belief in alternative narratives seems to be surging. If previous decades in the United States were defined by feelings of progress, ours is defined by a feeling of conspiracy, the last refuge of personal agency.

And what about Fitzpatrick and Reynolds's warning in their 1997 book, about people finding something worse than an MLM? In the mid-2000s, Donald Trump was the well-known spokesperson and promoter of the Trump Network and ACN, two large MLMs that no longer exist because of a number of lawsuits and fraud cases. ACN sold telecom equipment, including videophones and internet service. The Trump Network sold a series of vitamins. Trump explicitly viewed the Trump Network as a "rescue" program for those suffering from the 2008 recession. It was during Trump's stint that sales in both companies soared. After all, he possessed an uncanny ability to enrapture audiences and create community in a universe of alternative facts.

5.

On my mobile screen, a pale, ghostly woman is gyrating awkwardly in a pair of hot pants. Judging by her geographic location and the accent of her Mandarin, she's Han Chinese, with black hair and brown eyes, but she has put colored contacts in, which turn her eyes a strange tinge of blue. Her hair is dyed light brown. The lighting and video effects allow her to make her face look skinnier, the fashionable "snake-shaped face" (*shejinglian*, 蛇精脸) that turns her into an apparition. When she sits down to talk, her voice is high-pitched, each word ending in an evocative, cooing sigh, like she might pass out at any moment. Zhao points to her. "People like her. People think she's cool. That's the type of KOL [key opinion leader] we want wearing our pearls. Also Peng Liyuan, Xi Jinping's wife. We want her."

KOLs have been sprouting up all over China's internet in the past few years. While KOLs have long-standing "expertise" in some kind of subject matter, like lipstick or cars, a related category of online personas, *wanghong* (网红), has also appeared, as more generic influencers. KOLs and *wanghong* are everywhere on China's widely used video apps. In urban areas, KOLs are glossy Chinese equivalents of Instagram celebrities and influencers. Minimalist coffee shops, Prada purses, boho clothing, and red lipstick abound on Xiao Hong Shu (Little Red Book, 小红书), an app filled with shopping and lifestyle images. Between Guangzhou and San Francisco, there's an emerging global aesthetic of what it means to live a luxe life these days.

In rural China, KOLs and online influencers can be a peasant-style middle finger to the rest of urban China. Upper-middle-class urban China proclaims itself to be a society of high *suzhi* (素质), or civility, filled with soft-spoken white-collar workers who scroll through videos of people wearing *real* Zara blouses and their *real* Miu Miu heels to work. The rural livestreaming world is filled with *shanzhai* brands, people gyrating wildly to pounding electronic dance music, brothers debating the taste of bamboo rats, and welders nicknamed Baoding Edison creating inventions like a meat cleaver turned comb.

Lisa, Zhao's director of marketing, is a shy twenty-seven-year-old who is also from Zhao's home village. She left the village for college but ultimately came back, after her sister got into the rural e-commerce business and heard about Zhao. She says she learned most of her English from *Friends* and that she likes Lisa Kudrow a lot. She has large, dark-rimmed glasses that are constantly slipping down her nose and long bangs that cover her forehead. Her nails are coated with impeccable glossy gel that looks classy when she's holding a pearl bracelet. I learn from her how selling on rural livestreaming, which has become a conduit for getting rich, works.

Similar to Ren Qinsheng's costume business in Dinglou, Lisa uses Alibaba.com to sell bulk orders to overseas customers. Having just a few of these orders can yield a good profit, and establish a long-term business relationship.

To cater to the domestic Chinese consumer market, Lisa has a number of strategies. Livestreaming is one of them. Platforms and apps like Kuaishou (literally translated as "Fast Hands") feature people hawking all kinds of goods: oranges, glass beads, visits to a countryside home, and perfume, just to name a few.

There's also a whole contingent of livestream stars who make money as online idols. They perform, they sing, they have their own talk shows. Fans buy stickers (little icons that appear in the livestream window) for these livestream stars, worth a variety of amounts—anywhere from RMB 1 to RMB 10,000. These stickers come as roses or Ferraris, and fans gift the stickers to the stars in real time. Hosts can cash in the stickers they receive.

For people who make a living off livestream, the pressure to look a certain way is high. Some livestream stars get multiple plastic surgeries a year, and many aspiring stars will undertake drastic measures to achieve the much-desired snake-shaped face—large eyes and a pointy chin. The livestream industry is heavily gendered—women make up 70 percent of the industry as performers. Success is ultimately limited for the livestreamer, though, as livestream platforms can take up to 50 percent of a streamer's profits, and the emphasis on appearance favors younger stars.[3]

Livestream continues to be central across a range of new business models. Shopping sites like Taobao.com now incorporate livestream directly onto the platform. Other platforms like Kuaishou now have built-in stores. A far more personalized, addictive version of the home-shopping network, livestream blurs the line between selling a product and selling a feeling. A good seller builds an energetic rapport with the viewer, just like Kristie with her Krazy Kultured pearls.

The popularity of livestream is deeply tied to your income bracket. Few elite urbanites, whose lives are dictated by the rhythms of white-collar work, consistently watch livestream, although most will use the Douyin (TikTok) app to watch short, recorded videos.

Kuaishou's meteoric rise as one of the most popular apps in China is due precisely to its stronghold in rural areas. A large-scale study on Kuai by the anthropologist Chris Tan shows that Kuaishou's users are typically under twenty-five, without a college degree, living in rural or low-tier cities. They are usually unemployed or hold low-paying jobs, earning less than RMB 3,000 a month, as rural migrants or farmers.[4]

The popular Chinese press likes to fan the flames of Kuaishou's impact on rural society. For example: Zheng

Tao, a rural youth who left his village for factory work in a city.[5] A loser on the margins of urban life, he moved back home and became a livestream celebrity, making money from adoring fans. Other similar success stories have encouraged millions of youth to search for money and fame online. Chinese livestream's popularity echoes the same desires of American livestream, whether it's groups behind pearl parties or niche YouTube stars. The desire for community, for companionship, and, mostly, for monetizing emotions has never been stronger.

6.

Most of us know Peppa Pig as a British television cartoon pig for children, a little bit sassy but very cute. The Peppa Pig I'm looking at on my phone screen is smoking a cartoon cigarette and wearing sunglasses, being a bad, bad pig. On the official British cartoon, Peppa Pig would never smoke. She might occasionally be petty, but she's just a naive little pig learning how to be in *shehui*, in society.

Peppa Pig lives a double life in China. She's on cups and T-shirts, promoting delicious cookies for children and teaching kids how to be nice. On the internet, Peppa Pig is a rallying cry for disenfranchised youth. She is a meme, an online symbol for a growing group of people who believe the dominant system of society not only has no place for them, but also that, deep down, the system is rigged. Behind the memes of Peppa is not only a defeated irony but an anarchic embrace of "antisocial" behavior.

Peppa Pig is a symbol co-opted by *shehui ren*, a recent term coined on livestream, that translated literally means "society person." "Society person" describes the bulk of Kuai's demographic: people who are unable to live the shiny, upper-middle-class life promised to them in advertisements throughout China. While the transience of livestream and internet subculture gave rise to the Peppa Pig meme, the ethos her movement espouses is decidedly dangerous. Peppa's status as a subversive icon can be traced to one online short video in which someone displays a large back tattoo of Peppa Pig.

A movement coalesced around Peppa Pig, crystalizing a careless nihilism and rejection of mainstream values. Like in so many other countries, consumption has become the sacred value of daily life in China. The narrow path laid out by authority figures and parents is to get good grades to go to a good school, go to a good school to get a good job, and with a good job, shop, have kids, and shop some more. Instead of abiding by this prescribed life, *shehui ren* have no desire to enter the competitive whirl of school and employment; they see through the expectations of society. And the government sees this kind of nihilism as troubling, both socially and economically.

As a result, Peppa Pig memes were deemed lewd and inappropriate and subsequently removed as part of an "online cleanup" by government censors in the spring of 2018. Censors and state sources explicitly cited Peppa Pig's *shehui ren* culture as leading to antisocial behavior, "which could potentially hamper positive societal growth."[6] Fortunately, children were still allowed their beloved Peppa cartoon on official state channels.

This is the subversive potential of Peppa Pig memes and *shehui ren* culture. Videos from *shehui ren* still proliferate on livestream and other platforms. *Shehui ren* culture is not unique to China in its youthful anxiety about the future in a time of economic precariousness and astronomical housing prices worldwide. The glimmers of hope promised in the 1990s are now fading, with young people in China subject to enormous economic burden and only an illusory chance at the Chinese Dream. Many turn to Kuai as a place to bond and let off steam, and, for some, as a place to try to strike it rich as livestream stars.

One researcher, Yang Yuting at Beijing Normal University, has studied the culture of *shehui ren* in depth. Yuting explains that the Peppa Pig livestream meme was a culture developed around shared experiences throughout the country. With promises of middle-class stability unmet and increasing income inequality, young people rallied around the cry of "*Shehui, shehui!*" or "Society, society!" In everyday Chinese parlance, to be part of society (*rong dao shehui*, 融到社会) is what a moral, upstanding citizen desires. Online *shehui ren* culture parodied and mocked this normative sentiment. Yuting says that self-declared *shehui ren* are united against all the conventionally defined markers of being a good citizen. *Shehui ren* don't care about stable jobs, *shehui ren* don't care about the future, *shehui ren* are unproductive members of society, some refusing to get married and reproduce. For many *shehui ren*, a life or a business can be built on stealing or copying. *Shehui ren* live starkly against the everyday material life of glossy, happy ads on TV.

Street smarts are important for *shehui ren*—in order to *hun shehui*, or get by in society, as Zhao put it. *Hun shehui* involves stringing together jobs between the cracks of "respectable" society. From reselling fake Chanel perfume to livestreaming karaoke, there's nothing wrong with your chosen line of work when you're simply trying to live. *Shehui ren* are scoffed at by urban elites as crass and uneducated. But *shehui ren* couldn't care less what you think about them.

Despite the antisocial behavior of *shehui ren*, there remains the tinge of hope that if you can string together enough jobs, run enough scams, hustle hard enough, you can make enough money to become the boss of your own life, to play the system itself. Just like Zhao's dream.

In a small town outside of Chengdu, I make friends with a woman named Nicly who runs several housing rentals. She's eager to become friends with me because I'm American, maybe wealthy, and maybe I could bring her business. Every day she sends me a sticker on WeChat, calling me *jie* (姐, sister). I page through her WeChat and her Kuaishou. She is a *shehui ren*, her livestream feed filled with videos of face masks she's selling. Clicking through, I find one video where she talks about her current hustles and how others can learn from her. Sometimes *hun shehui* is more important than school, she says. It's lame and boring to just go to school and hope you're going to get somewhere through conventional means. Plus, the chances are low: those who are already well-off had well-off parents. It's better to rely on yourself and your street smarts. She tells everyone that she used her street smarts, and last year she managed to buy a car. The video has 1.2 million likes.

7.

In my hand, I hold a can of formaldehyde with a dead oyster floating inside. Before I leave Zhuji, Lisa explains the process for making a wish pearl. First, a large triangle mussel is inoculated with small plastic balls. A coat of lacquer is allowed to form over a year—much less than the standard five years for a quality pearl. Each triangle mussel produces thirty to forty pearls. Since the excitement of a pearl party is in the opening up of an oyster that has one or maybe two pearls, the pearl farm takes small, cheap oysters, opens them up, and transfers one of the original pearls from the large mussel into the smaller oyster. This small oyster is now a wish oyster. Lisa told me that if I wanted, I could custom order pearls to be dyed all sorts of colors before being inserted into the smaller oyster. This is because pearl party hostesses often like to announce what each pearl color symbolizes—luck, happiness, or friendship. Each oyster is worth less than RMB 5.

Shipping is a drag, explains Lisa. One method the companies in Zhuji have been trying is vacuum sealing the small oysters individually. Before vacuum sealing, the oysters are soaked in formaldehyde, a slightly carcinogenic chemical that stings and smells bad, preserving the dead flesh and preventing rot. Another chemical, which Lisa doesn't remember the name of, is used to make sure that the small oysters remain closed—after all, an open oyster signals a dead oyster, and the whole point of a pearl party is to shuck ones that *look* alive. While vacuum sealing has been successful in cutting down on shipping costs, the weight of hundreds of oysters leads to occasional crushing. Another method is to ship the oysters in cans of formaldehyde. Kristie's Krazy Kultured Pearl Parties uses oysters preserved by this method, I observe, as one evening Kristie remarks that her hands sting from the stinky oysters. I can't smell through the screen, and that's probably why this pearl party illusion through livestream works so well.

I know there are other things I can't tell through the screen, but I'm tempted to buy one, just to hear Kristie say my name, to wish me happiness and joy, to watch the screen fill with comments congratulating me on my pearl-chase. I wonder if Kristie knows where the pearl came from, what she thinks of Zhuji, of China in general. During one party, over the awkwardness of video, she stares blankly into the screen, seemingly unaware of being broadcast, wearing a pearl necklace. She's wide-eyed, with skillfully applied makeup, the kind of makeup I wish I had the talent to do.

In Lee Edelman's book *No Future: Queer Theory and the Death Drive*, he provokes readers to think about a set of impossible politics, a theory of failure. While conventional politics are defined as the push and pull between the left and right, he insists that most of us end up creating a culture where political action is premised on the illusory figure of "the Child." The call to act is haunted by the specter of "our children," whether it is a future of environmental destruction or a disorderly future without "traditional values." We are always trying to live for the child that does not yet exist, fixing the world for our children who do, impressing our expectations on their desires. These political visions draw upon fears of decline or loss of control, on an innate need to crave a future—some kind of story or meaning that motivates us to keep living. This same need is the reason why we get stuck in a cycle of chasing after the future, a future that never appears as perfect as we imagined it to be.

The only way out, Edelman suggests, is to declare an end to the future—a rallying cry for "no future." By definition, it's a kind of release, perhaps a Buddhist nirvana.

The future has been sold to all of us, not just the *shehui ren* of Facebook Live or Chinese Kuai, as a lottery, a glint of happiness or a threat of catastrophe. And while I don't see myself as a *shehui ren* who pushes against the broader system, the more livestream I watch, the more I wonder: What is the point of respectability, of living for imagined futures? Figures prance across my phone screen: young men in the countryside of China, elderly grandparents with no teeth watching their grandsons moonwalk and sell acne cream. Kristie singing another round of "Like a Pearl-Gin." Desire and future becoming one, into a desperation I can feel.

I think of my parents, my grandparents. My grandmother and her nightmares, how the last few years of her life were marked by her confronting the depth of her past, despite having lived for the future in her youth. My mother's insistence on a better life, as she defined it, full of expectations for her children's future that neither my sister nor I was able to fulfill. Her fingertips, cracked and dry from working, saving for a life that she felt was not hers. Why do I work long days to dutifully pay off the five-figure student debt I have, the debt I took on in fantasizing about a better life? Even if I paid off the debt, would the debt-free future that awaited me be as perfect as I imagine?

I think I keep showing up every day for the same reason Kristie and Nicly do. A sense of purpose, a sense of being needed. A community, no matter how small. I dutifully take the BART ride from the East Bay to San Francisco every day, to a beautifully generic office filled with standing desks and Aeron chairs. I show up despite knowing that the only thing my time and labor amount to is making rich men richer. The best parts of work are the interactions with other people, and even conflict gives a sense of community. I spend more time with my coworkers than with friends or partners. My daily life is either sleeping or working. It's like having a family, but I wonder if this is the family I would actively choose. And on evening BART rides back home, I listen to music in my headphones, watching other people with startup-logo-embroidered backpacks scroll vigorously on their phones, smirking and laughing at the screens. I am still left with a sense of loneliness. Kristie's next pearl party awaits me at home, along with a box of Green Chef and some packages from online New Age boutiques.

Maybe that's just a microcosm of the difficult work that we want to skip: the work of building a community upheld by boundlessness and belonging, a sense of purpose beyond reducing work and life to simple economics. I think of the Peppa Pig meme and how strong a new community's culture can grow, aided by symbols. It's easy to mistake the power of the Peppa Pig meme as simply resulting from the internet. But culture and community, not technology, are the driving force behind its power, its threat to the elite. As internet researchers such as An Xiao Mina and sociologists have shown, the driving force behind broader sociopolitical change has always been culture, with or without the internet.[7] Cultural change comes before political change, and that cultural change starts with us. It is up to us to make meaning, to make new symbols.

In recent years, visioning exercises have come into vogue. The internet is saturated with these little moments. The idea behind this visioning is simple. If you just close your eyes and imagine your future in great detail, you will manifest it. In this kind of magical-thinking exercise, the word "manifest" seems easy, as if your dream of more money, more friends, and fame will just suddenly come into existence.

One of the memes circulated on a Facebook pearl group says, in a quirky cursive font: "Close your eyes, think of the future, what do you see?"

Instead of dreaming of the happy day when I'll have paid off all my student debt, the happy day when doctors manage to find a cure for my progressive, incurable disease, the happy day when I've saved up millions to buy a house in the San Francisco Bay Area, I am exhausted trying to conjure a blurry future. A dream that is peddled as a future filled with total ease.

A few days before the start of a new decade, I sit at a quiet terrace bar in Hong Kong as dusk falls. The city has become a world of strange contrasts, with riot police standing guard outside cosmetic stores as people buy mascara, and police violence against protesters in luxury shopping malls. Banks and stores associated with the Chinese government have been shuttered; storefronts protectively shrouded in plaster are covered in protest graffiti. Reports of a new zoonotic disease from mainland China causing flu-like symptoms in humans has added to the city's unease, the memory of SARS still recent. The tropical air smells faintly sweet, laden with the figures of Hong Kong's colonial past and the decline of empire. I try the exercise posted on the Facebook page. I close my eyes. Stillness washes over me, like embers that quietly glow in the middle of this restive metropolis.

I stare into the darkness that shifts with occasional washes of light. I cannot bring myself to see the honeyed visions of a comfortable future. Instead, I see the intrinsic truth of living as one of difficulty, the constant effluent of change. Without a future, I must give myself over to the present, to undertaking the work that must be done.

It's easy in the moments of stillness, somewhere between getting home exhausted and opening up my laptop again to watch *yet another video*, to sense that there are other paths. I sense there is something past ardent nationalism and total technological bliss, something past endless scrolls and lonely rage, past the floating world and ceaseless talk that skims across the surface like foam. Both nationalism and technological optimism mark the ways yearning and desire are exploited. They fall away in stillness. Governments drum up nationalist support, promising stability and control over our futures. Tech companies capitalize on this nationalism. Sunny ads promise frictionless prediction and control, a reassuring probability of a safe world, where refrigerators can order food delivery and happiness is guaranteed forever. A new strain of tech progressivism is equally insistent in our political and social lives, promising that, if we can only efficiently scale up our political actions and movements, if we can only optimize our good deeds, we will achieve the future that *we* all want. It's that easy. But I am less curious about this stifling singularity and more curious about the revealed state of "interbeing": a term the Buddhist monk Thich Nhat Hanh uses to replace the simple binary of being and nonbeing.

I continue to stare. The present stares back. The present moment promises nothing—it only demands. It demands building the communities that shift culture, that allow interbeing to thrive. It demands the *work* of awareness and care, instead of the *tools* of efficiency and scale. It demands seeing individual freedom as nothing more than a way for all of us to be oppressed. Most of all, the present demands the tender, honest work of attempting to make meaning, instead of looking, waiting, or wanting. Through the present moment I see the glimmers of liberation embedded in the work we must do at this time. Because what else can we do?

Notes

1. Ghosts in the Machine

1. Kakuzo Okakura, *The Book of Tea* (Digireads.com, 2019).
2. Yasheng Huang, *Capitalism with Chinese Characteristics: Entrepreneurship and the State* (New York: Cambridge University Press, 2010).
3. Zhihong Zhang, "Rural Industrialization in China: From Backyard Furnaces to Township and Village Enterprises," *East Asia* 17, no. 3 (September 1999): 61–87.
4. Eric Holt-Giménez, "Part 1: The Agrarian Transition," interview by Tracy Frisch, EcoFarming Daily, https://www.ecofarmingdaily.com/the-agrarian-transition/.
5. C. Cindy Fan, "Why Rural Chinese Are in No Rush to Settle in Cities," *Nikkei Asian Review*, July 27, 2017, https://asia.nikkei.com/Economy/C.-Cindy-Fan-Why-rural-Chinese-are-in-no-rush-to-settle-in-cities. See also: The Institute, Inc., "The Chinese State, Local Communities, and Rural Economic Development," special issue, *Urban Anthropology and Studies of Cultural Systems and World Economic Development* 41, no. 2/3/4 (Summer/Fall/Winter 2012).
6. An Chen, "How Has the Abolition of Agricultural Taxes Transformed Village Governance in China? Evidence from Agricultural Regions," *The China Quarterly* 219 (2014), 715–35, https://doi.org/10.1017/S030574101400071X.

2. On a Blockchain Chicken Farm in the Middle of Nowhere

1. For more information, see Guobin Yang, "Contesting Food Safety in the Chinese Media: Between Hegemony and Counter-Hegemony," *The China Quarterly* 214 (May 9, 2013), https://doi.org/10.1017/S0305741013000386.
2. 韩长赋, "任何时候都不能忽视农业忘记农民淡漠农村（深入学习贯彻习近平同志系列重要讲话精神)," *Renmin Daily*, August 13, 2015, http://web.archive.org/web/20170223093119/http://politics.people.com.cn/n/2015/0813/c1001-27453126.html.
3. 黄哲程, "探索区块链在食品安全领域的运用, 新京报," *Beijing News*, November 4, 2019, http://web.archive.org/web/20200317213627/http://www.xinhuanet.com/food/2019-11/04/c_1125189022.htm.
4. Kenneth G. Lieberthal and Michel Oksenberg, *Policy Making in China: Leaders, Structures, and Processes* (Princeton, NJ: Princeton University Press, 1988).
5. "Garrett Hardin," Southern Poverty Law Center, https://www.splcenter.org/fighting-hate/extremist-files/individual/garrett-hardin.
6. Similar concepts, like "survival of the fittest," based on Darwin's ideas of natural selection, give scientific credence to economic systems like capitalism—with its aggressive emphasis on competition. Survival of the fittest has been similarly disproven. The biologist Lynn Margulis has shown that the major driving force behind evolution is symbiosis, not natural selection.

3. When AI Farms Pigs

1. 付永军, "痛心 | 洋猪入侵中国30年: 正在爆发一场生态灾难, 31种土猪已濒临灭绝!," 原乡味觉, December 6, 2018, https://web.archive.org/web/20191231224046/https://mp.weixin.qq.com/s/auURR08y2mIW6cc9lexKlQ; Vincent ter Beek, "ASF China: Kitchen Waste Blamed; Outbreaks in the South," Pig Progress, October 29, 2018, http://web.archive.org/web/20191231224754/https://www.pigprogress.net/Health/Articles/2018/10/ASF-China-Kitchen-waste

-blamed-outbreaks-in-the-south-352451E/; Ann Hess, "ASF Prevention: Should Meat Be Removed from Garbage Feeding?," National Hog Farmer, November 2, 2018, http://web.archive.org/web/20181102201534/https://www.nationalhogfarmer.com/business/asf-prevention-should-meat-be-removed-garbage-feeding.

2. "Chinese Tech Companies Get into Farming," *The Economist*, October 27, 2018, http://www.economist.com/business/2018/10/27/chinese-tech-companies-get-into-farming.
3. Dipendra Thapaliya, Blake M. Hanson, Ashley Kates, Cassandra A. Klostermann, Rajeshwari Nair, Shylo E. Wardyn, and Tara C. Smith, "Zoonotic Diseases of Swine: Food-Borne and Occupational Aspects of Infection," in *Zoonoses—Infections Affecting Humans and Animals*, ed. Andreas Sing (Dordrecht, Netherlands: Springer, 2015), 23–68.
4. Henry A. Kissinger, Eric Schmidt, and Daniel Huttenlocher, "The Metamorphosis," *The Atlantic*, August 2019, https://www.theatlantic.com/magazine/archive/2019/08/henry-kissinger-the-metamorphosis-ai/592771/.
5. Sylvia Wynter, "Unsettling the Coloniality of Being/Power/Truth/Freedom: Towards the Human, After Man, Its Overrepresentation—an Argument," *CR: The New Centennial Review* 3, no. 3 (Fall 2003): 257–337, https://doi.org/10.1353/ncr.2004.0015.
6. Terry Winograd and Fernando Flores, *Understanding Computers and Cognition: A New Foundation for Design* (Boston: Addison-Wesley, 2008), 106.
7. Audre Lorde, "Poetry Is Not a Luxury," in *Sister Outsider: Essays and Speeches* (New York: Crossing Press, 2007).
8. Audre Lorde and Adrienne Rich, "An Interview with Audre Lorde," *Signs* 6, no. 4 (1981): 713–36, https://www.jstor.org/stable/3173739.
9. Lorde, "Poetry Is Not a Luxury."
10. Rodrigo Ochigame, "The Invention of Ethical AI," *The Intercept*, December 20, 2019, https://theintercept.com/2019/12/20/mit-ethical-ai-artificial-intelligence/.

11. James Boggs, "Blacks in the Cities: Agenda for the 70s," *The Black Scholar* 4, no. 3 (November 1972): 50–61, https://doi.org/10.1080/00064246.1972.11431284.

4. Buffet Life

1. 程盟超, "这块屏幕可能改变命运," 中国青年报 (*China Youth Daily*), December 18, 2018, http://web.archive.org/web/20190329013258/https://mp.weixin.qq.com/s/l4f4r2d7bw06mqBstJL-mA.

5. Made in China

1. Ruth Oldenziel, *Making Technology Masculine: Men, Women, and Modern Machines in America, 1870–1945* (Amsterdam: Amsterdam University Press, 2011).
2. Buck Gee and Denise Peck, "Asian Americans Are the Least Likely Group in the U.S. to Be Promoted to Management," *Harvard Business Review*, May 31, 2018, http://web.archive.org/web/20200107032025/https://hbr.org/2018/05/asian-americans-are-the-least-likely-group-in-the-u-s-to-be-promoted-to-management.

Analyses of intellectual property and law as ways to control culture are plentiful, including Lawrence Lessig's work. Susan Sell, "Intellectual Property and Public Policy in Historical Perspective: Contestation and Settlement," *Loyola of Los Angeles Review* 38 (Fall 2004), http://web.archive.org/web/20200108180433/http://digitalcommons.lmu.edu/cgi/viewcontent.cgi?article=2452&context=llr; William W. Fisher III, "The Growth of Intellectual Property: A History of the Ownership of Ideas in the United States," *Eigentumskulturen im Vergleich* (Göttingen, Germany: Vandenhoeck & Ruprecht, 1999), 265–91, http://web.archive.org/web/20181116052143/https://cyber.harvard.edu/property/history.html.

6. "No One Can Predict the Future"

1. For a good read on this, see Zhang Xi, "'Cake Uncles': Formation of a Criminal Town in Rural China," *Crime and the*

Chinese Dream, ed. Børge Bakken (Hong Kong: Hong Kong University Press, 2018).

2. Ruth Wilson Gilmore, *Golden Gulag: Prisons, Surplus, Crisis, and Opposition in Globalizing California* (Berkeley: University of California Press, 2018), 5–29.
3. Zara Rahman, "Can Data Ever Know Who We Really Are?" Deep Dives, May 16, 2019, http://web.archive.org/web/20190528233256/https://deepdives.in/can-data-ever-know-who-we-really-are-a0dbfb5a87a0.
4. For more, including a fairly fascinating takedown of some common health "data," see Philip B. Stark, "Quantifauxcation" (PowerPoint presentation, European Commission Joint Research Centre, Ispra, Italy, January 19, 2015), https://www.stat.berkeley.edu/~stark/Seminars/fauxIspra15.htm.
5. Ruha Benjamin, *Race After Technology: Abolitionist Tools for the New Jim Code* (Cambridge, UK: Polity, 2019).
6. Frantz Fanon, *Black Skin, White Masks* (New York: Penguin Classics, 2019).

7. Gone Shopping in the Mountain Stronghold

1. See Melinda Cooper, *Family Values* (Brooklyn: Zone Books, 2017), for an in-depth analysis of how traditional family values work in a neoliberal era.
2. Lauren Berlant, "Lauren Berlant on Her Book *Cruel Optimism*," *Rorotoko*, June 4, 2012, http://web.archive.org/web/20190617083541/http://rorotoko.com/interview/20120605_berlant_lauren_on_cruel_optimism/.
3. Agence France-Presse, "How China's Young People Became Addicted to Debt," *South China Morning Post*, May 28, 2017, http://web.archive.org/web/20180114200736/http://www.scmp.com/news/china/economy/article/2096019/how-chinas-young-people-became-addicted-debt.
4. "China's Moon Mission Sees First Seeds Sprout," BBC News, January 15, 2019, www.bbc.com/news/world-asia-china-46873526.
5. Chang'e is the Chinese goddess of the moon.

8. Welcome to My Pearl Party

1. 薇宋, "The Annual Debate on Heating in China," *China Daily*, http://web.archive.org/web/20191111090652/http://www.chinadaily.com.cn/china/2015-01/30/content_19449162.htm.
2. Zhuang Pinghui, "As Winter Grips Rural China, Who's Really Paying the Price for Beijing's Clean Air Plan?," *South China Morning Post*, January 24, 2019, http://web.archive.org/web/20191221164917/https://www.scmp.com/news/china/politics/article/2182521/winter-grips-rural-china-whos-really-paying-price-beijings-clean.
3. Peter Yang, "A Primer on China's Live Streaming Market," *Hacker Noon*, July 21, 2018, https://hackernoon.com/a-primer-on-chinas-live-streaming-market-352409ad2c0b.
4. Zhang Bo, "The Performers Behind China's Much-Derided Livestreaming App," *Sixth Tone*, December 21, 2017, http://web.archive.org/web/20191023080549/http://www.sixthtone.com/news/1001437/the-performers-behind-chinas-much-derided-livestreaming-app.
5. 董志成, "Streaming out of Shanty Towns for Bigger Dreams," *China Daily*, http://web.archive.org/web/20190220043533/www.chinadaily.com.cn/hkedition/2018-12/21/content_37415794.htm.
6. Shan Jie, "Chinese Video App Removes Peppa Pig, Now a Subculture Icon in China," *Global Times*, April 30, 2018, http://web.archive.org/web/20190102130006/www.globaltimes.cn/content/1100136.shtml.
7. An Xiao Mina, *Memes to Movements: How the World's Most Viral Media Is Changing Social Protest and Power* (Boston: Beacon Press, 2019). For an academic study on this, see Damian J. Ruck, Luke J. Matthews, Thanos Kyritsis, Quentin D. Atkinson, and R. Alexander Bentley, "The Cultural Foundations of Modern Democracies," *Nature Human Behaviour* (December 2019), https://doi.org/10.1038/s41562-019-0769-1.

Acknowledgments

This book's journey has been marked by so much kindness and compassion, from people and places too numerous to name. Any omission in this list is purely accidental.

Thank you, *Logic* family: Alex Blasdel, Celine Nguyen, Christa Hartsock, Jen Kagan, Jim Fingal, and especially Ben Tarnoff and Moira Weigel. Thank you, Emily Bell, Jackson Howard, Rebecca Caine, and everyone at FSG Originals for bringing this book to life.

I am enormously grateful to the interviewees who spoke with me and the communities that welcomed me; thank you for your insights and candor. For reading drafts and giving generous feedback and encouragement, thank you: Carl Tashian, Martabel Wasserman, Jane Henderson, Siyu Song, Alexander Arroyo, Dorothy Santos, Josh Feola, and especially my sister, Jen Wang. Thank you, Maya Rudolph, for your commitment to adventure. An enormous thanks to Yang Yuting for all your assistance in arranging interviews, and for your critical astonishment at the state of rural America. For conversations and support that have influenced this book's trajectory, thank you: Abigail de Kosnik, David Li, Joyce Lee, Hetty McKinnon, LinYee Yuan, Sharad Chari, Jovan Lewis, Hallie Chen, Sam Culp,

Kira Simon-Kennedy, Pinghui Xiao, An Xiao Mina, Jason Li (who came up with the title!), Nicole Lavelle and Charlie Macquarie of Place Talks, Meg and Rick Prelinger, Shane Slattery-Quintanilla, Xinran Yuan, Angel Chen, Alex Chow, Jordan Maseng for the noodles, Deren Guler, Bing Bin, Grace Zhou, Leafan Rosen, Alatanwula for the horses, and Shazeda Ahmed for Christmas in Hangzhou. Thanks to everyone at B4BEL4B Gallery, World Wide West, Andres Colmenares and Lucy Black-Swan, and the Miracle Swimming group at North Beach Pool. I am grateful to the community of Zhaoxing, Guizhou, for much-needed ghost visitations and witchcraft during writing. Thank you to my former coworkers at Mapbox, where parts of this book started to percolate—particularly to Amy Lee Walton, who encouraged me to write more, Vanessa Frontiero, and Jake Pruitt. And thank you, Helen Mirra, for your wisdom and walks, which teach me to "let go, let go, let go."

This book would not be possible without my aunt and uncle, Victor Wang and Jacqueline Chen, who gave me their unwavering support and a home in Guangzhou. Thank you to my mother, who continues to diligently feed people in the middle of a global pandemic, and to my grandmother, who remains ever present in my life. And Ian Pearce: I am always grateful for your patience, support, and endless good humor.

The intellectual and spiritual influences of this book are many. Yet it all began with the cookbooks and food writings of Buwei Chao, M.F.K. Fisher, Jessica B. Harris, Mary Sia, and Alice B. Toklas. I am still studying and practicing all your recipes.